GORDON ADLER

Financial Times Briefing on
Management Communication

To Mark
All the best to you
Gordon

Financial Times
Prentice Hall
is an imprint of

PEARSON

Harlow, England • London • New York • Boston • San Francisco • Toronto • Sydney • Singapore • Hong Kong
Tokyo • Seoul • Taipei • New Delhi • Cape Town • Madrid • Mexico City • Amsterdam • Munich • Paris • Milan

PEARSON EDUCATION LIMITED

Edinburgh Gate
Harlow CM20 2JE
Tel: +44(0)1279 623623
Fax: +44(0)1279 431059
Website: www.pearsoned.co.uk

First published in Great Britain in 2011

ISBN: 978-0-273-73637-0

British Library Cataloguing-in-Publication Data
A catalogue record for this book is available from the British Library

Library of Congress Cataloging-in-Publication Data
A catalog record for this book is available from the Library of Congress

10 9 8 7 6 5 4 3 2 1
14 13 12 11 10

Typeset in 9.25 Swiss 721 BT by 30
Printed and bound in Great Britain by Ashford Colour Press Ltd, Gosport, Hampshire

FAST ANSWERS TO CRITICAL BUSINESS DECISIONS

As a high-performance leader you need to tackle pressing business issues and deliver hard measurable results. *Financial Times Briefings* give you the targeted advice you need to:

- get to grips with business critical issues quickly
- develop a solutions-focused mindset
- ask the right questions
- take the right actions
- measure the right things
- make the right decisions.

Key features include:

- Clear, concise information
- A focus on actions and objectives rather than theory
- Brief, relevant case studies of success stories and failures
- Benchmarks and metrics to gauge outcomes and achievements
- Briefing Lessons to distil key business insights

Financial Times Briefings *series advisors:*

- Jim Champy, author of bestselling business book *Reengineering the Corporation* and Chairman Emeritus, Consulting, Dell Services
- Rob Grimshaw, Managing Director of FT.com
- David Macleod, co-author of the MacLeod report on employee engagement and non-executive director at MOJ and DfID
- John Mullins, Professor at London Business School
- Sir Eric Peacock, Non-Executive with the DTI, a board Member of the Foreign and Commonwealth Office Public Diplomacy Board and Chairman of 'What If' – rated by the FT as the No. 1 company to work for in the UK
- Kai Peters, Dean of Ashridge Business School
- Simon Waldman, Group Product Director at LOVEFiLM

Contents

To Sylvia, who taught me how to listen, connect with others and build rapport, day in and day out – skills that have served me well as a manager.

[PART ONE]

In brief

Executive summary

1

Introduction

The typical employees of a global financial services organisation are on the receiving end of around five internal news bulletins and newsletters, endless corporate email messages, mission statements posted in hallways and common meeting areas, desk drop cards with lists of company values, posters littered with values statements, numerous video presentations, blogs both written and video, and voice mail phone-in systems for daily recorded messages from divisional heads. That's a lot of 'communication'. Despite the fact that management experts and consultants will tell you that regular, frequent, targeted communication is good, in the corporate world morale is relatively low, and communication is described as 'needs improvement'. Communication often leaves a lot to be desired.

In research I conducted over five years[1] into the communication behaviours and skills of senior managers in large, international companies, the following came to light:

- Only *one* respondent in *ten* expressed the belief that managers know how to communicate corporate messages effectively.
- More than half said that their managers don't spend enough time communicating with their employees.
- Six out of ten described their managers at all levels as 'out of touch'.
- Eight out of ten believe that the communications skills across their executive teams could be improved.

Oddly, almost 72 per cent said that managers in their companies see employee communication with employees as critical to company success, but that effective communication is 'rarely taken as a priority'. As one interviewee put it: 'Our managers are too concerned with hitting their numbers, meeting their targets, boosting the bottom line and generally holding up their end of the "corporate deal", to invest the time, effort and energy to improve their personal communication skills and their communications with employees, to say nothing about communicating with their publics.'

What's going on here?

With the exponential increase in communication media (email, short messaging, Twitter, social networking sites) and the increasing volume of communication every employee and stakeholder must deal with in our highly wired, online, digital society, managers are, in the words of an HR manager at the global pharmaceutical

---

[1] 'Storytelling in Management Communication: an exploratory study', Doctoral thesis, University of South Australia, International Graduate School of Business Administration, Division of Business and Enterprise, July 2006.

company Novartis International, based in Switzerland, 'snowed under, caught in an avalanche of emails and voice mails, trapped in hours of mind-numbing PowerPoint presentations, with the nagging sense of being "behind" and "short of breath"'.[2] Given the speed of interactions, business objectives, tactics and budgets are often revised. With a scandalous headline or a downward tick in the stock price, the rules you work with can change. Increased transparency means that your work is apt to be discovered and scrutinised by more and more people.

You face more and more distractions. You and your employees are interrupted more often, more insistently and in many ways. Questions reverberate in your head: have you read and answered all your email? Caught up with reports? Scanned the headlines and dealt with your voice mail? In this environment it's almost impossible to stay focused or hold the attention of people around you.

Even if you've found ways to stay focused, you are asked to get and hold the attention of people around you without annoying, boring or disrupting them. Considering how many demands your stakeholders face, being respectful of their time and becoming a priority only when appropriate are essential to keeping trust and confidence. The 'good old days' of 'I talk, you listen' are gone.

Today, you may be working across organisations, management chains and continents. You wouldn't call a friend at two in the morning, but you may have been guilty of scheduling a meeting that forced someone in another time zone to get out of bed. More often than not, you will have team members on the other side of the world or spread across the globe. How do you communicate with them effectively? How do you engage them, work toward common interests or even get to know them personally? Since effective communication is two-way, how do you maintain connections and make yourself available?

Management communication is unique

Management communication is different from other kinds of communication. That's because in a business or management setting, a well-written or artful message alone is insufficient: you succeed only if your message gets the response you want from your audience. To elicit that audience response, you need to think strategically about all your communication, and communicate in a reliable, compact and meaningful way (for the audience).

To communicate more strategically, you need to make effective communications choices. To make these choices, you need a simple way to think about them. One easy way is to divide up the many communications activities that you and your company face into three groups of related activities:

- interpersonal communication,
- company employee communication, and
- company external communication.

[2] Ibid.

You need all three, and you probably have a management role in at least the first two.

For each of the three groups of communications activities, there is one basic three-step model you can follow. Making effective communication choices in each of the three areas of management communication entails a three-step approach:

1 Prepare your communication.
2 Send your message(s).
3 Check for understanding.

If you follow these steps purposefully for every one of your communications, whether one-on-one interpersonal communication or company-wide external communication campaigns, you and your company will improve your communications.

What is management communication?

- What is communication?

- The process of communication

- What is *management* communication?

What is communication?

Before we define management communication, we need to define communication. Ask a group of managers for a definition of communication and you'll get many answers, for example:

- inform
- clarify
- share knowledge
- develop ideas
- understand
- explain
- persuade
- socialise
- develop relationships, and many more.

For our purposes, effective communication is sharing information in an easily understandable way. Success is getting the response you desire.

If a manager speaks, and the employees don't understand, is that communication? Of course not, you say. But it happens every day.

Take a moment to think about what you use communication for at work, and how many times a week you use it for that purpose. The purposes for which you use communication say a lot about you and your values; they reveal your personality and reflect your management style. Complete the frequency of communication matrix.

Frequency of communication matrix

Purpose	Times per week				
	0	1	2	3	4+
Better understand a colleague					
Clarify an idea or plan					
Build rapport, improve relations with a colleague					
Gain credibility					
Show competence or expertise					
Persuade someone					
Share information					
Explain something (strategy, rationale)					
Tell someone how to do something					
Inspire someone					
Share a moment of silence					
Resolve conflict, deal with negative emotion					
Set goals					
Run a meeting					
Show colleagues how their work impacts mine					
Express thanks or appreciation					
Ask someone to do something					
Bring humour into a situation					
Make a presentation					
Send an SMS or MMS					
Write an email					
Deliver a town hall, webinar or webcast					

Reflect for a moment on these questions:

1 Do you use communication more for one purpose than for another?
2 Which purposes do you prefer?
3 Where do you need to communicate more often? Why?
4 What can you conclude about your communication uses?
5 Does this mini-audit reveal any issues?

Now imagine how your colleagues view you as a communicator. The following questions will help you become even more aware of how your audience may perceive you:

1 What would my work team members or colleagues say about my communication habits?
2 What would they say I use communication for primarily?
3 What would my manager/boss/leader say about my communication habits?
4 What would they say I use communication for primarily?
5 What are the discrepancies between your view of your own communication use and those of people who observe you regularly at work? What can you conclude from this discrepancy?
6 What areas do you want or need to work on in your management communication?

The process of communication

Communication is a process. Its main components are: communicator, receiver, filters (the hindrances to communication), message, filters (again), feedback and background noise or interference. Figure 2.1 shows a simple model:

Figure 2.1 A simple model of communication

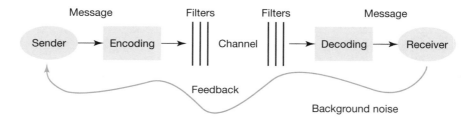

We communicate in many ways: with words, tone of voice, facial expressions, physical gestures, dress and even how we use space (where we stand in conversations, how our offices look). The sender is the encoder and the receiver is the decoder. In any face-to-face interaction, this encoding and decoding happens thousands of times. For example, you can ask, 'What did you do today?' in many ways. Each carries a different meaning:

- ***What*** did you do today?
- What ***did*** you do today?
- What did ***you*** do today?
- What did you ***do*** today?
- What did you do ***today?***

Communication happens on many levels. The obvious meaning of the words makes up the text, which is the information or the data in the message. For example, 'Please stop by my office today at 3 p.m.' The underlying meaning of the message, the subtext, is what makes you wonder if you're in trouble with your boss, going to get a pat on the back or should make an excuse not to go. The *subtext* is usually communicated through feelings. Threats, dissatisfaction, appreciation, enthusiasm, humour – most emotional content – is communicated through subtext, especially in business, where there are often unspoken taboos against expressing feelings openly. Sometimes we misread the subtext of a message because we, as listeners, make assumptions about the speaker or the message. You might assume, for example, that your boss emailed you because he's impatient or wants to check your work because he distrusts you. But your boss may have another reason: the chairman of the board sent him an email asking for the project plan.

Our aim is understanding, which amounts to this: accurately encoding and decoding both the content (text) and the intention (subtext) of a message. Every message you send goes from information through understanding to acceptance or rejection (see Figure 2.2).

Figure 2.2 The process of understanding

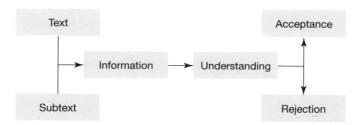

In simple terms, communication comprises three basic steps:

1 Prepare yourself and the receiver (audience).
2 Send your message.
3 Check for understanding.

There is clearly much room for things to go wrong! Many obstacles block or distort communication: making assumptions and judgements, conflicting values or beliefs, incongruent words and body language, incompatible styles, failure to listen, even misunderstandings about the meanings of the words themselves.

> To counter these obstacles, there are things you can do to improve communication: build rapport, share a common goal, use a language of shared meanings, active listening, clarifying assumptions, using an assertive style, matching your communication style to the context, making your words and body language congruent, paraphrasing, summarising, and many more.

Management communication is successful only if your message results in getting the desired response from your audience, so you need to think about your communication, not as a straight line from the sender to the receiver, but rather, as a loop (or many continuous loops) (see Figure 2.3).

Figure 2.3 The communications loop

What is *management* communication?

The overriding purpose of most management communication is to get people to do something. After all, management is really about getting things done or, rather, getting people to get things done. Management communication is a persuasive campaign – much like a political campaign, although you are seeking results, not votes.

Ask a room full of managers, 'What is management communication?' and you get all sorts of answers:

- marketing communication
- corporate communication
- business communication
- public relations
- leadership communication
- leading teams
- email, and so on.

This is a reflection of the widespread uncertainty about these terms and functions, both in companies and in the world of communication scholarship.

Years ago, everything was all much simpler. Managers recognised only one business communication need: whether selling, telling, persuading or seducing, business communication was about introducing products and services to the market. So management communication was company communication: externally focused, top-down, customer-driven and pretty much one-way.

But then came technology and globalisation. Business speeded up and rapid change became a constant. In the world of work, commitment replaced compliance. Knowledge took centre stage. Hierarchies gave way to flat, networked organisations. Processes and relationships became more important than formal structures. Where reason and logic had always held sway, stories took on a new importance. In communication terms, the one-way, one-dimensional, broadcast view of communication gave way to two-way forms of communication: dialogue, conversations with customers, social networking platforms and online communities. Suddenly, all managers were responsible for communication.

This changing view of company communication was fuelled by problems outside companies. Remember the major 1970s PR disasters? Shell's Brent Spar crisis, Exxon's Valdez oil spill or Coca-Cola's Belgian misstep. For the first time, these companies needed more help than their PR experts could offer. A 'new' corporate communications function sprang up: 'crisis management'. In crisis management, it became a truism that 'it's not what you say, it's what people hear'.[1] Audience-centred communication took on a new importance. Since the mid-1990s, many companies have embraced the communications function. They work to orchestrate all their communications activities in four communication areas:

- internal identity
- external reputation
- corporate branding, and
- management of communication.

[1] From the title of the book, *Words That Work: It's Not What You Say, It's What People Hear*, by Dr. Frank Luntz, Hyperion, New York, 2007.

Many try to tie together all these activities through a corporate 'story'. And most have swung the focus of their attention from what they want to say to what they want their audience to understand. This is a subtle, yet significant change.

There seems to be an increasing awareness that communication in general and managers' communication responsibilities in particular are extremely important in a company's strategy process and implementation. Despite this rising awareness, some business schools do not even teach strategic management communication to senior executives. Many managers ignore communication, or at least do not communicate purposefully, figuring that others will take care of it. Many companies do not allow their communications experts a seat at the strategy table. If you're looking to learn how to align your own communications with the company's strategy and implementation activities, you'll have to look long and hard for advice or best practice. Given the importance of communication, this lack of awareness or commitment is starting to look like a dereliction of duty.

So what is the definition of management communication? Even the definition is unresolved. There is little agreement. Many of the definitions that managers use are actually not definitions of management communication. They include corporate communication, management communication, strategic communication, business communication and organisational communication.

Management communication is the communication of managers on various levels with various target groups, internal and external. These target groups can be single employees, entire departments or the public in general. For some managers, management communication is whatever the communications department does: internal and external communication, company communication, marketing communication, corporate communication, sponsoring, investor relations, job market communication, issues management, even PR. But this book treats it as what managers themselves do when they communicate with internal and external audiences.

Management communication is a mixture of one-on-one communication all the way to communications with external stakeholders. However, focusing too much on the individual tasks of presentation skills, media training techniques and interpersonal skills will not make you automatically a better communicator.

Effective management communicators recognise that good communicating involves:

- dialogue
- asking open questions
- deep listening
- building rapport
- co-creating, not telling
- knowing yourself: authenticity
- genuine enthusiasm and commitment
- knowing your style
- knowing your audience
- clarity, conciseness and consistency.

Corporate communication can mean public relations, corporate advertising and advocacy, media relations, public affairs, investor relations, environment communication, corporate advertising, internal communication, financial communication, employee relations and communication, community relations and philanthropy, government relations, crisis communication, corporate branding, reputation and strategy-setting. Different companies give different tasks to their corporate communications departments. Basically, corporate communication is the orchestration of all the instruments in the field of organisational identity (communication, symbols and behaviour of organisational members) to create or maintain a positive reputation with groups with which the organisation has an interdependent relationship. So, the purpose is to build competitive advantage for the firm.

Marketing communication is concerned with various forms of communication that support sales: advertising, direct mail, personal sales, brochures, sponsoring, etc. These activities are aimed directly at the customer. But communications aimed at improving a company's reputation (like indirect sales promotions) are often called organisational communication.

Business communication is normally viewed as a subject for undergraduates and MBAs, and is focused on skills, especially writing. Business communication takes a micro view of the communicator's daily business tasks (mainly writing) rather than a macro, or strategic, view of communications. Where corporate communication focuses on the *entire function* of management, business communication turns its lens on the communicators themselves, with a focus on skills (later in this book, we call this the 'interpersonal communication sphere').

Management communication is all the communication managers must do to communicate effectively in their organisations: from the individual to the corporate level. From traditional written and spoken forms to computer graphic-generated presentations, from email to press conferences and web pages on the internet, the effective manager must communicate with brevity and clarity. While the number of channels for communication in business rapidly increases, the ability to persuade and motivate has never been more important. This book looks at this dynamic field, and, together with a variety of electives, examines topics such as crisis management, corporate reputation, organisational identity and technology, managing professional communication as well as the challenges of effectively communicating across societal, global, and organisational boundaries. Each manager and every company has a story to tell – management communication makes sure that that story becomes a competitive advantage.

Communication is situational. It is shaped by the profile of the manager or leader and the profile of the employees, the situation in which the communication takes place, the nature of the audience and the culture of the company where the communication happens. The key question about the communication is: did it work?

> **The key ingredient of effective management communication is not the medium, the process or a particular action, it is the tools you use to communicate effectively in the situation in which the communication takes place.**

Briefing Lessons

Management communication is the sharing of information in an easily understandable way. It includes all the communication managers must do to be effective in their organisations, including:

- **writing, speaking and presenting**
- **email, SMS and MMS**
- **blogging, social networking**
- **meetings, town halls, webcasts and press conferences**
- **websites, marketing, sales and branding activities.**

Management communication has four parts:

1 **the communicator**
2 **the message**
3 **the receiver**
4 **the response.**

These four parts comprise a *process* that happens on many levels (for example, text and subtext), not in a straight line from sender to receiver, but in loops of rapid feedback. Management communication is unique: you are successful only when your message gets the desired response from the receiver, only when it is understood as you intended it and then accepted by the receiver.

Many obstacles hinder management communication. To overcome them, managers should think about communication as conscious, purposeful choices that lead to saying the right thing to the right people in the right way at the right time – all in the name of getting the desired result.

Why management communication?

3

- Why bother?
- Costs
- Rewards

Why bother?

Every day you go to the office and face a long list of tasks and responsibilities. You try your best to meet them with the tools you've got – and you try to follow your principles. All the while, the phone rings, email arrives, people drop by your office, meetings take place, you give presentations, countless small matters demand your attention. You are trapped in a web of communication. You are too busy trying to meet your goals and targets to give enough thought to effective communication. You'd like to, but other things keep taking your attention. And besides, communication seems like a such big, amorphous subject… you don't know how to talk about it, or measure it.

You and your equally busy employees have a deal with your company: The company gives you a job, a desk, a regular pay cheque, an organisation, people and, if you're lucky, the chance to develop yourself. In return, you give your company your time, your energy, your commitment and loyalty, your ideas and your performance. You spend your days discussing with people. Convincing people. Persuading them. Explaining. Even deciding against people. So your management deal involves relationships: interactions. It is never one-sided. Employees aren't coin-operated Japanese robots you throw money into and get action. You need loyalty. Loyalty is based on trust, and trust depends on communication.

In earlier times, you could follow these principles:

- guide and control employees
- one-way, criticism-free communication
- the manager is the guardian of knowledge
- hierarchy wins over complexity.

But today, you're confronting demands for:

- teamwork
- permanent communication
- risk and opportunity management
- innovation
- multi-cultural management and cross-border M&A activity
- knowledge sharing, valuing and developing the strength of others
- motivation and engagement
- open work spaces and collaboration
- respect for the work–life balance
- commitment to dialogue, conflict resolution
- emotions, creativity and non-conformity.

To meet these requirements, you need effective communication. It isn't enough to be a skilled number cruncher or an ace project manager. To become one of the best managers in your company, or simply to advance your career, you must master the art of communication, or the process in which individuals interact, exchange and interpret meanings. Merely conveying information through idle chitchat and smartphone emails is easy. Communicating effectively requires skill, intent and finesse. You need to be able to present ideas effectively, persuasively, clearly and concisely. You need to engender trust, motivate, build confidence, fuel innovation and lead people through hugely disruptive change. Good communication matters because business organisations are made up of people. As Robert Kent, former dean of Harvard Business School has said, 'In business, communication is everything.'

Research spanning several decades has consistently ranked communication skills as crucial for managers. Typically, managers spend 75–80 per cent of their time engaged in some form of written or oral communication. Although often termed a 'soft' skill, communication in a business organisation provides the critical link between core functions. Here are four reasons good communication is important to managers and their companies.

Reason 1: Ineffective communication is very costly

Communication in a business provides the critical link between core functions. The US National Commission on Writing estimates that American businesses spend $3.1 billion annually just training people to write. People who cannot write and communicate clearly will not be hired, and if already working, are unlikely to last long enough to be considered for promotion. Eighty per cent or more of the companies in the services and the finance, insurance and real estate sectors – the corporations with greatest employment growth potential – assess written skills during hiring.

Bob Kerrey, president of New School University in New York and chair of the National Commission on Writing, suggested that writing is both a 'marker' of high-skill, high-wage, professional work and a 'gatekeeper' with clear equity implications. People unable to express themselves clearly in writing limit their opportunities for professional, salaried employment.[1] The ability to communicate was rated as the most important factor in making a manager 'promotable' by subscribers to *Harvard Business Review*.[2]

[1] 'A Ticket to Work… Or a Ticket Out; A survey of Business Leaders', Report on the National Commission on Writing, For America's Families, Schools and Colleges, College Endurance Examination Board, September 2004.
[2] 'Proven Methods for Effective Communication', Amit Salkar, www.ezinearticles.com

Reason 2: The increasing complexity of the 21st century workplace makes management communication even more important

Flatter organisations, a more diverse employee base and greater use of teams have all made communication essential to organisational success. In flatter organisations, managers must communicate with many people over whom they may have no formal control. The days when a manager can just order his or her employees around are finished. The autocratic management model of past generations is being replaced by participatory management in which communication is the key to building trust, promoting understanding and empowering and motivating others.

Because the workforce is growing more diverse, a company can no longer assume its employee constituencies are homogeneous. Employees are different in age, ethnic heritage, race, physical abilities, gender and sexual orientation. Diversity is not just a matter of social responsibility, it is also an economic issue. Companies are realising the advantage of making full use of the creativity, talents, experiences and perspectives of a diverse employee base. But this advantage rests on effective communication.

Teams are the *modus operandi* of the 21st century workplace, and they are all about communication. The collaboration that allows companies to capitalise on the creative potential of a diverse workforce depends on communication.

Reason 3: The world's economy is becoming increasingly global

From 1966 to 2002, the direct investment of foreign-based companies in the United States grew from $9 trillion in 1966 to more than $300 trillion in 2002. Many products people assume are American, such as Purina Dog Chow and Kit Kat bars, are made outside America. Brands we may think are international, Grey Poupon mustard, Michelin tyres and Evian water, are made in the United States.

Reason 4: Our brains are hard-wired signal processing machines

Neuroscience provides insight into why managers need to be concerned about how they communicate. In terms of brain science, the decoding of messages is essentially the interpretation of signals by the receiver's mind. The mind processes information by simplifying it. So, the simpler the messages our brains receive, the more easily our brains can process it. Our brains like structure, so we need our messages in structured language, with ideas organised in logical groups and structured narratives, with key messages and rhetorical patterns that accommodate our biases and deliver information that suits our needs. The brain is also hard-wired to process emotions. The rational part of the brain is blocked when the emotional centre of the brain is occupied. When emotions run high, especially fear, the best rational or logical information will neither engage nor persuade receivers. Many managers underestimate the power of fear and other emotions in communication. A good example is the ineffectiveness of logical arguments to convince employees to commit to a major change programme.

No surprise, then, that experts regard management communication as one of the most important management skills. Managers, depending on their functions and levels in the organisation, spend up to 80 per cent of their time communicating with employees, customers, staff, investors, the media and other stakeholders. Effective communication skills are tantamount to success for companies.

 Tip

To be effective, communication channels need to be open down, up, and throughout the organisation.

Managers have been called the most powerful communication channel. Manager communications have an impact on brand, employee morale and even share price. Subordinates take cues on how to communicate from managers. Managers who are good communicators get more from their direct reports than managers whose strong skills lie elsewhere. Managers are the insurance policy for keeping the best workers happy. The way you communicate (or don't!) reflects your management style, company and national culture and values. So, it is likely to affect the performance of the people you manage, your ability to make change happen and perhaps your ability to recruit and retain top people.

There is much talk today about the importance of values: sustainability, integrity, trust, openness, respect, courage, responsibility, to name a few. You cannot build and sustain any of these without communicating effectively. Good communication brings clarity, boosts confidence and develops trust and commitment. Poor communication confuses, disillusions and demotivates. How would you rate your own communication in your organisation? A source of clarity and commitment or of confusion and opting out? What's your communication style? Personal and energetic or formal, jargon riddled and stolid?

Costs

The costs of poor management communication are hard to measure. Communication isn't a typical management function. That's because communication is the *means* by which managers achieve their tasks. Without communication, there cannot be any management. Without effective communication, management is ineffective.

Inconsistent or weak communication:

- confuses stakeholders
- sabotages careers
- hurts employee morale
- hurts company reputations
- lowers sales
- ruins change projects
- destroys morale
- disillusions customers
- makes bad news on the internet
- creates bottlenecks in your company
- drives away talented employees
- creates a media feeding frenzy.

Rewards

The rewards of effective communication are many and varied and a few common ones are:

- higher management credibility
- higher trust and better rapport among employees
- higher engagement
- more productive teams
- clearer objectives
- more productive dialogue
- fewer conflicts
- wider knowledge sharing
- more efficient problem solving
- faster innovation
- quicker strategy formulation
- successful change programmes
- more satisfied customers and investors
- wider understanding of the company vision, mission and story
- stronger brand, better reputation
- higher revenues.

Briefing Lessons

There are a number of compelling reasons to improve your communication, including the following:

- According to decades of research, communication ranks high on the list of crucial skills for managers.
- Managers typically spend up to 80 per cent of their time communicating.
- Although management communication is not a business function, it is essential: without communication, there can be no management.
- Managers are one of a company's most powerful communication channels: management communication has an impact on brand, reputation, employee morale and performance – even share price.
- In today's flat, high-speed, widely dispersed organisations, managers need the loyalty, trust and credibility they get from effective communication.
- Ineffective communication is expensive, in time and money.
- The increasing globalisation, complexity, virtualisation and unpredictability of the workplace make management communication more important than ever.
- Our brains like structure, simplicity and visualisation: they process information by simplifying and structuring it, so simple, clear communications are easier to process.

Who's doing it? Including two short case studies

4

- Case study 1: Success

- Case study 2: Failure

Case Study 1: Success

Jürgen Dormann's 'Friday Letters'

 Throughout the economic boom of the 1990s, the Swiss company ABB expanded its operations rapidly. This is the same ABB that, in 2009, won a $70 million power order for London Underground and a power transmission order worth $550 million from the Irish grid operator. But back in 2002, before its many newsworthy projects in the UK and around Europe, ABB was being crushed under a mountain of debt and recorded a loss of US$ 787 million. The group's portfolio was said to be too broad and too complex for its resources: it needed to be simplified. Enter Jürgen Dormann, new chairman and chief executive, who, with board and top management support, embarked on a radical cost-cutting exercise and started to streamline operations through a major restructuring.

A major part of the group's restructuring translated into large-scale job losses. Announced in late 2002, the cost-cutting programme aimed to cut the annual cost base of the company by $900 million by mid-2004. ABB announced that the number of jobs being cut under the austerity programme would be between 10,000 and 12,000. In addition many others would be leaving the ABB fold through a programme of divestments, which meant that a company that employed 140,000 people in 2002 would have around 100,000 employees at the start of 2004.

By 2004, at the end of this painful change, the six business divisions that existed in 2002 had been cut to two core divisions – Power Technologies and Automation Technologies (with a third division, Oil, Gas and Petrochemicals, in the process of being divested). The debt had been slashed resulting in ABB being one of the world's leading producers of industrial robots. Analysts pronounced that an air of confidence had returned to ABB as the company continued to put in place measures to strengthen its focus and finances.

As part of this major change programme, ABB placed a good deal of weight on increasing communications and transparency, both internally and externally. With a new focus on communication, Jürgen Dormann wrote employees a no-frills weekly letter, published on the company's intranet, which was designed to build employee trust in the company. In itself, nothing special. CEOs send letters and emails every day. But the process that followed is a prime example of how any company should design and run a crisis and change communication campaign.

After that first posted letter in 2002, Dormann sent one every Friday to all ABB employees – in 12 languages. The letters communicated openly and honestly where ABB stood and what direction management was taking. Dormann believed in open communication. His aim was to ensure dialogue with employees, invite their input and bypass traditional layers of hierarchy. He wanted to cover key topics, to create certainty where there was uncertainty and to show the way forward despite the many hurdles that stood in ABB's way. More specifically, Dorman wrote in his final letter, on 22 December 2004, that he was trying to make sure everybody in ABB understood drastic action was unavoidable.

Through his letters, Dormann conveyed his views honestly and offered facts, with full transparency. This guaranteed that all employees – no matter in which country or which department they worked – knew exactly where their company stood. Even more important was that the Friday letters also took on an important feedback function – employees could respond and share their concerns or comments. Astoundingly, Jürgen Dormann read all the answers – a total of 4,500 responses in two years – and took up the points raised week by week in his next letter. Employees merely had to click on a 'Feedback' button to know that their CEO was listening carefully to all employees. The letters show, in Dormann's words, 'how one troubled industrial company rose to meet its challenges'. The key point here is that plain speaking and plain listening went hand in hand, and over time dialogue developed.

Dormann's actions give us a list of key leadership traits that all communicators would do well to heed.

 Tip

- **Operate with complete integrity.** Keep your word, and do the right thing – even if you are the only one who knows you are doing it.
- **Become an expert in your field.** 'Expert power' provides one of the major sources of authority because people follow those who 'know their stuff'.
- **Tell people what you expect.** Use clear language to describe goals, values and expected behaviour. Develop a plan, and act on it. Listen for feedback that may signal the need for a change in tactics, or even in strategy.
- **Mean it when you commit.** You'll inspire people if you show them you accept the risks that commitment brings. You do that by sticking to your path in adversity and solving problems that seem impossible to others.
- **Expect the best.** Maintain a self-confident vision of what you want – success – not a negative view of what you don't want – possible failure. Positive thinking has power, but only if you fuel it with enthusiasm.
- **Care for those you lead.** Put their needs at the top of your priority list. If things go wrong, 'take' two things – charge and responsibility. And when things go right, share two things – the recognition and the rewards.
- **Put others first.** Think of those you lead before yourself. Celebrate their success by giving them as much credit as possible. And share their pain even if it is inconvenient, difficult or costly in time, money or other resources.
- **Do what the word 'lead' implies – get out in front.** If you're not willing to do what you ask your people to do, don't ask them to do it.

- **Play to your own strengths.** Learn how to compensate your weaknesses. Let your team members understand how you rely on them, and why. Don't assume you know everything, or that you are always right.
- **Keep a sense of perspective.** Strive for broad-based solutions. Take the time to resolve differences. No one gains if you leave wreckage in your path.

Source: Dormann, J. (2004) 'The Thank You Letter, 22 December 2004', *The Dorman Letters*, ABB.

Case Study 2: Failure

Crisis communication: the communication glitch at Toyota

In the early spring of 2010, in the US, the Toyota company recalled 133,000 Prius hybrids and 14,500 Lexus HS250h cars to fix faulty brakes. Soon after Toyota would recall some 200,000 cars in the UK because of a safety scare over the accelerator pedal. Similar problems in Toyota cars across the world would lead to the recall of millions of cars in total. This bad news came hard on the heels of other bad news: two other problems with the cars were said to cause unintended acceleration. In all, over the span of two months, Toyota recalled about 8.5 million cars for safety reasons. There has been much debate in the media about the causes of these problems – Toyota's supply chain, its reluctance to engage, its insular culture – but one glaring dilemma reported by many regarding the recall has been Toyota's response to the series of recalls. The issue, as countless crisis communications experts have pointed out in tweets, blogs and interviews, is that Toyota didn't anticipate the impact the recalls would have and failed to take control of the communications situation raised by the recalls. Toyota appeared to allow the story of its recalls to fester, responding slowly to the issues and delaying communication with customers and other stakeholders, instead of finding ways to resolve the issues so it could focus on regaining the public's trust. As problems mounted, and the media got interested, Toyota appeared to simply react, instead of taking command of the deteriorating communication situation.

The first word about problems with the Prius brakes came out when regulators in Japan and the US said they were investigating the vehicles. Had Toyota communicated more effectively, they would have told the public immediately that the company had identified a problem with the car's brakes, instead of leaving the early communication to safety officials. The consequence was extensive negative news coverage and internet comment. There was so much information and misinformation on public forums that Toyota lost the opportunity to become the definitive source of information. The company's delay in communicating became a part of the crisis itself. To make matters worse, when Toyota finally spoke, it said that it had fixed the brakes of cars coming off the assembly line, but that it did not yet have a fix for customers who already owned a Prius. The problem stemmed from a software glitch that caused about a one-second delay before the anti-lock brakes kicked in on bumpy or slick roads.

Toyota waited one full week to announce a recall of the Prius. Although experts note that Toyota reacted as fast as it could to fix the problem, coming up with a fix that is tested and reliable takes some time. The company could have announced a recall before it had finished testing its software update, but it chose to wait until it had the fix in place. Once the recall was announced, sales dropped 16 per cent in the following weeks.

Was this a poor communication choice? Frustrations among Prius owners ran high, flamed by what many articles called Toyota's 'inept' response. When the company announced the recall, but did not have a customer fix ready, it should have stopped selling the Prius. This is exactly what the company had done with its recall of the Camry and Corolla models, which had been plagued by sticky accelerator pedals. In those cases, Toyota stopped selling the cars until its dealers had the parts necessary to fix them.

When Toyota announced the sticky gas pedal problem a few weeks after the Prius software glitch, the company had learned its communication lesson and, in the minds of experts and cable news commentators, was doing a solid job of reassuring customers that it had fixed the sticky gas pedal problem. This was a strong communications start but, by then, Toyota had squandered an excellent opportunity. Despite its quick reaction to the sticky brakes and speedy reassurances, Toyota did not manage to demonstrate, beyond a shadow of a doubt, at least in the public's perception, its technical reliability.

It seems clear, in retrospect, that some of Toyota's short-term decisions were poor. Naturally, consumers want an instant recall and an instant fix. Toyota's communication team should have anticipated this desire, and done a better job staying ahead of the story, which spread across the fields of the blogosphere faster than a bush fire.

For many, the question remained why a simple software upgrade to fix the brake problem could have taken a week. In the minds of consumers, the computer 'glitch' was really about safety and the lives of their children and loved ones. Communication couldn't have been fast enough.

What can we learn from the Toyota case? For one, no matter who you are, a multibillion dollar company with a premium brand or a small non-profit, there are certain communication truths that govern almost any crisis.

Tip

- If you or your organisation is in crisis, you need to communicate immediately. If you don't communicate quickly, you make the crisis worse, because the media get their information, not from you, but elsewhere.
- Your response to any crisis changes the crisis. A brilliant response to a crisis almost always leads to better media coverage (a slow, lacklustre response almost always generates worse coverage).
- The media always focus on the victims. The media and the public almost always see a crisis from the perspective of the victims.
- Lastly, burying bad news rarely works; in fact, it often broadens and deepens the crisis. The news gets out anyway, and any appearance of dishonesty or cover-up cements any suspicions people have about an organisation's forthrightness.

 Briefing Lessons

This chapter examined effective interpersonal and employee communication at the Swiss company, ABB, and problems in external communication at Toyota.

The key briefing lesons we can learn from the ABB case are as follows:

- In times of major restructuring, downsizing, crisis and change, employee communication needs to be an ongoing persuasive campaign, frequent and transparent.
- Over two years, ABB's CEO, Jürgen Dormann, wrote a weekly, no-frills newsletter to all employees that openly and honestly communicated the company's challenges, position and direction, promoted dialogue and signalled that Dormann was willing to listen. The letters quickly took on a feedback function: over two years, employees responded with 4,500 comments.

And the key briefing lessons from the Toyota case are as follows:

- In spring 2010, Toyota recalled about 8.5 million cars around the world for safety issues. The company's communication response allowed the story of its problems to fester and grow longer than it should have.
- After the story of the Prius brake failures broke, Toyota waited a week to announce a recall. Not communicating immediately and taking command of the messaging was a mistake. Burying bad news rarely works. Toyota's response to the crisis worsened it.
- Toyota failed to understand that the media nearly always focused on the victims.

[PART TWO]

In practice

How to manage communications: a step-by-step guide

Management communication is a big, complex field. It isn't rational, or formulaic. So, we need a simple way to think about it. The simple way to think about the various activities that fall under 'management communication' is to imagine three 'spheres' of communication. Each sphere is defined by the group to which you are communicating:

- The interpersonal communications sphere: individual interpersonal management and employee communication
- The internal communications sphere: internal, employee and marketing communication
- The external communications sphere: communication with external stakeholders (e.g. corporate affairs, lobbying and media).

The three spheres of communication

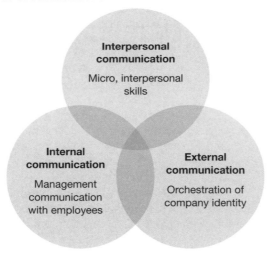

Sphere	Skills required and activities
Interpersonal sphere	Interpersonal manager communication skills
Internal sphere	Employee communication Internal communication
External sphere	Marketing communication Corporate affairs, lobbying Media communication

In order to master all three spheres of management communication a manager must, among many things:

- understand how the communication process works
- make purposeful strategic communications choices
- think of communication as a three-step process
- have good writing, dialogue, public speaking and presentation skills
- know how to use non-verbal communication
- have a certain degree of communication charisma
- be able to empathise with the audience and connect.

Chapter 5 will consider the interpersonal sphere; then the following two chapters will address internal and external communication.

Interpersonal communication

5

- The three-step model

- Step 1: Prepare yourself and the receiver

- Step 2: Send your message

- Step 3: Check for understanding

- Prepare a personal strategic communication action plan

The three-step model

The main components of any communication, whether one-on-one between a manager and an associate, or between a company and its multiple stakeholders, are:

- communicator
- receiver
- message
- feedback (response).

It is useful, therefore, to imagine communication as a three-step model (see Figure 5.1).

Figure 5.1 Communication as a three-step model

Prepare yourself and the receiver → Send the message → Check for understanding

Within each of the three steps there are many factors you need to take account of in order to improve your chances of communicating effectively. Within each step, you've got many chances either to make your communication more effective or to create obstacles that hinder shared understanding. Assume that your message will be ineffective if the receiver fails to understand it in the way you meant it. Your aim as a sender and their aim as a receiver is the same: mutual understanding. That is not to say you need agreement, but rather, that the message is understood.

Step 1: Prepare yourself and the receiver

Preparing yourself need not take long. I'm not advocating that you carry around a two-page checklist and review it before you hit the send button. But spending a few seconds to get clear on a few key concerns such as your purpose, the message, how you can present it optimally to your audience before you communicate may save you time in the long run.

 Tip

Remember: everything you do or say, or don't do or say, sends a message. Effective communicators need to be on their toes. Managers who communicate effectively consider all their communications as strategic. It's a matter of choosing the right message for the right people in the right way at the right time, but always in alignment with company strategy and messages. Communication strategy is communication choice.

You can do much to prepare your audience for your communication, but you cannot control their reactions. Conversations, as we all know, may not go exactly as planned. You need to remain flexible and open throughout the process. You need to want to communicate. And your heart needs to be in it.

To form the basis of any strong communication, you need to reflect on four areas:

1 **Your goal.** What you should communicate.
2 **Your audience.** Who you plan to communicate with.
3 **The channel.** How you will communicate.
4 **The key messages.** What you would like to get across.

The first three areas are considered next while the key messages will be considered in Step 2.

1 Your goal

Many communication books and courses give you a long list of possible communication purposes. Here's an example:

	Move	Brief	Connect
	Direct	Inform	Motivate
PERSUADE	Focus	Clarify	Instruct
	Sell	Entertain	Lead
	Communicate	Inspire	Humour

Why is **PERSUADE** in bold font? Most management communication is ultimately about persuading someone. You give instructions, inform people, pass on information and knowledge, ask questions with the overriding goal of getting things done. So management communication is about moving the company toward its goals.

Use the grid below to practise articulating your purpose with any audience.

2 Your audience

Your audience comprises the person or people you're communicating with. They are the 'receivers' of your message. In business, it is often a group with similar interests, needs or demands – under similar circumstances. Before you create your message, give some thought to what you want them to think, feel, believe and do. I maintain that, since business is about getting things done, the key question here is what do you want the audience to do?

What do you want the audience to *think*?	What do you want the audience to *believe*?
What do you want the audience to *feel*?	What do you want the audience to *do*?

When you 'define' your audience, look at them from the point of view of their interest in what you're saying (or writing). Instead of thinking about what you would like to say, think about what they should take away, remember and therefore *do*.

Ask yourself:

- Is it relevant to them?
- Does it have consequences for them?
- Will they care?
- What is their situation/predicament – the state of their mind or feelings – today?
- What's in it for them?

One way to determine your audience groups is by their level of knowledge. Another way is by their position in the company hierarchy. Other factors that you might include are education, origin, culture, gender and age. These are all 'filters' that may impede your communication, the factors that may prevent your audience from receiving your message as you intended.

 Tip

If you are going to deliver your message face-to-face, before you communicate, try to be sure that the person with whom you are communicating is ready to hear you. If you're not sure, ask them:

- **Is this a good time to talk?**
- **Can we discuss something I have in mind?**
- **Would this be a good time, or should we make an appointment for later?**

3 The channel: how will you communicate?

The single greatest thing I learned while managing a communications department was the power of assuming positive intent. I had an employee who was literally 'pushed' onto my team by my boss, who wanted to avoid a wrongful dismissal law suit. At first, I was very angry about my boss's actions, and had a very poor first conversation with the employee, who needed the job but didn't seem any more happy to be working for me than I was having her on the team. I assumed that if she was entangled in a potential dismissal issue, she must be difficult to work with, and not especially open to working for me.

But by assuming positive intent, on the advice of a colleague, I let the employee know that I wanted to make things better and that I cared about doing the right thing. I stopped assuming that she was difficult, or was trying to mess things up because of our bad start. Although we never got much beyond a cool formality in our dealings, she was very bright and quickly became one of the best, most reliable people on the team.

 Amy, a senior manager, once had a boss with whom she frequently had conversations that she felt went badly because she thought he was 'in a bad mood' or was 'dumping on her'. Her boss, Mark, once told her, with no clear explanation, that a website project had not gone the way he expected, even though he had signed it off (there were cost overruns and some of his management colleagues were unhappy with the proposed design) and that she 'had egg all over her face'. Amy could see he was in a foul mood, and assumed it might be because of the project, but also that other factors could be in play (a health issue in his family and other thorny management challenges that were frustrating him).

Needless to say, Amy was neither open to Mark's criticism nor amenable to his suggestions. To Amy his intentions were unclear. Was he trying to berate her? Blame her? Get her to do something? Make him feel better? To this day, the meaning of their conversation remains clouded. It left Amy with negative impressions and a lot of anger. Had Mark wanted a constructive solution to the project problem, he should have practised positive intent. He should have assumed that Amy had good reasons for doing what she had done and saying the things she'd said to his management colleagues when showing them the web design. But Mark seemed to be assuming that Amy had negative intentions, or didn't have a sound rationale for her decisions. With his negative moods, he thus created with Amy – and many others – a destructive environment. This made it impossible for Amy and her colleagues to work in a constructive, cooperative way. Often, in meetings Mark treated them as though he assumed they were stupid, incompetent, slow and generally out of touch with what 'really mattered'. A favourite phrase was, 'You just don't get it.'

What do the voices in your head tell you? Do they have the voice of an overly critical teacher? Do you have a voice in your head that whispers, 'This is never going to work.' 'You don't get it.' 'You're not smart enough.'

I have taught myself to think that behaviours or feelings I encounter, no matter how odd or strange they may seem to me, may have some useful and important positive purpose, particularly from the perspective of the other person. You can take this too far, assuming, like Candide, that 'everything is for the best' when someone else is plotting your downfall, badmouthing you or sabotaging your work, but this not what I'm advocating.

> ### 👍 Tip
>
> **Just make sure that your self-talk isn't negative. As Diogenes once said, 'If your mind isn't open, keep your mouth shut, too.'**

Prepare yourself: tame your inner critic

Think about the evaluations and the assumptions you make routinely about people, situations and events. How do they help/hinder your communication? We all tend to look for evidence to confirm our assumptions, rather than being objective in our evaluations. Remember the Pygmalion principle: the leader's expectations often determine the employees' or teams' behaviour.

Assumptions lead to attributing motivation to the actions of others. The fundamental attribution error, simply put, is: when I do something it's because I understand the situation, have considered all the options and decided the situation really calls for my particular solution. When you do the same general thing, it's because you don't really understand the situation, are short-sighted and have no idea how damaging your act is to others.

Self-talk is the term for all the things you say to yourself during the day. It's the wordy turmoil below the calmest demeanour. It is how you describe yourself, the people around you and the world. It is like a frame around your picture of life. Self-talk is another filter for coding and encoding your messages, and can be a large barrier to effective communication.

This inner critic may be useful. It may spur you on to greater achievements and better performance. But it may also hamper you, hurt your relationships and hinder your performance. For some people, the inner critic is so powerful that it stops them from ever trying anything. Actors talk a lot about the inner critic, and relate it to stage fright.

Stage fright is common to presenters. But it can also affect all our communications. Without even being aware of it, we may be making a difficult communication situation – for example, a critical performance review – even worse by having negative thoughts about it before, during and after. Think about what you say when you talk to yourself:

- No way I'm paid enough to put up with this rubbish.
- My manager is an idiot.
- It's not my damned fault!
- This is the most boring meeting ever.
- I'm fat!
- I'm never going to make it.

What you tell yourself about situations and people frequently determines, or at least plays a strong role in, how you act around them or react to what they do or say. This means that you will be a more effective communicator if you are aware of your self-talk. Much of this self-talk flows out of assumptions about ourselves, or about the person or communication situation we are in.

Think about the internal messages you tell yourself that either help or hinder your ability to communicate. List three of them below – a couple of examples are provided to get you started.

Topic	Message you tell yourself (your self-talk)
Example	This is never going to work the way I want it to.
Example	This meeting is a waste of time: what a bunch of incompetent idiots.

Much of our inner criticism is based on assumptions we make about people. That's only natural; after all, we are curious, pattern-forming creatures. We look for intelligible forms and sequences, interpretations and explanations – even if they are wrong, and based on faulty assumptions. We have an experience, assume similarities with previous or next experiences, and then we attribute cause and motivation to it. We tend to look for evidence that confirms our assumptions, rather than being objective (as objective as we can be) in our evaluations. Although our inner talk may be helpful, it is not always useful. It can become a strength that quickly turns into a weakness if we are not aware of our assumptions.

- What assumptions do you hold about the people you manage?
- What assumptions do they have about you?
- How do these assumptions manifest themselves in your communications?
- What effect do they have on your team's or department's performance?

Try making this even more specific. Think back to a recent conversation at work that was about an important issue or project. Use the following table to identify the assumptions and evaluations. Again an example is provided to get you thinking.

What was said	What I assumed
We need this finished by Friday.	If I get the project done by Friday, my boss will be satisfied.
	or
	He says this because he doubts that I will make it and he wants to cover his bets.
	or
	He knows I can't get it done by Friday, so he wants me to look bad in front of Friday's meeting. He's setting me up to fail.
	Or
	It's just a routine, habitual reminder. He does this all the time. It's part of his self-talk – but out loud.
	Or
	He's afraid he'll look bad at the meeting, so he's preparing to sandbag me.

Is your self-talk useful to you in your management communications? In what way is it not useful? To prepare for your next management conversation, complete the following exercise (and compare your answer with the sample provided).

Subject or person	**Dr Wilson, CEO**
My assumption(s) about it	He always looks for what doesn't work, and all the ways the people in the meeting have failed to live up to his standards.
How it affects me and other people	My assumption that Dr Wilson is over-critical causes me to panic and speak poorly in meetings. It causes others to be defensive and usually on the lookout for criticism. This results in people keeping their ideas and suggestions to themselves.

Prepare yourself: be aware of your power, credibility and influence

The effect of power on you and your receiver

Power is the capacity to get things done. The most common kind of power in a company is positional power: the power that comes from holding a title or sitting in a certain position within the organisation chart. Other kinds of power are:

- **Association power:** from membership of a group.
- **Influence power:** the power that comes from who listens to whom.
- **Credibility power:** the power of reputation.
- **Knowledge or expertise power:** from learning or a great skill.
- **Resource power:** from staff, equipment and money.

Where do people in companies get their power? No one is actually wearing a crown, and few companies require uniforms where ranks are indicated by stripes on their sleeves. Even in such companies, a man with many stripes may have less power than a man with few stripes who has other kinds of power. Different companies, temperaments, cultures, ages and genders give more credence, deference or unquestioning respect to other members of the organisation merely because of the type of power relationship they have.

With each kind of power come certain culturally defined status, perks and treatment. When you communicate with someone who has a different degree of power, there are all sorts of expectations about what you can say, or not say, and how you can say it. If you get this wrong with a person who has a different level of power, you may quickly be facing some ugly consequences, especially in companies and cultures that are high on the power–distance scale.

 Tip

To communicate effectively with people who hold different kinds of power, you should ask yourself what influence the various kinds of power have on your communication. Use the table below to help you.

Type of power	Its influence on me
Power of position/title	
Power of association	
Influence power	
Credibility power	
Knowledge power	
Resource power	
Other power	

The effect of credibility on you and your receiver

People in certain positions of authority expect a certain behaviour, and therefore a certain style of communication, from you and the others around them. When they get it, they tend to give the person who demonstrated it more credibility. Credibility has been called the 'invisible currency' in organisations. When you hear someone make a statement, you check the source and decode the message based on your assessment of the source's credibility. Credibility is what makes each of us believable. If your communication is perceived as appropriate to your power status, people will give you more credibility.

- Do you have credibility with the people in positional power in your company?
- How did you earn it?
- How could you lose it?
- Does your communication build your credibility, or diminish it?
- How can you build your credibility with your communication?

If you want to guard your credibility, you need to be careful not to overuse the word 'no'. Nothing undermines credibility more than overusing the word 'no'. If you're always negative, you are likely to lose your credibility – and hence, your influence – with people. Almost any phrase can be recast with a positive 'spin'.

Negative phrase	Your positive version
No.	Here's what I *can* do for you…
I can't.	I can…
No way we'll do that.	We could consider…
That's not company policy.	Here's how we usually deal with that…
That's not my problem.	(Edith) can help you…
It's not my fault.	Let's try to fix this…
Calm down.	I understand your frustration…
I'm busy now.	Could we chat at 3 pm?
Call me back later.	When can I call you back?
I have no idea.	Let me find out for you.
The data base lost your information.	Here's the information I have…
You're wrong.	Let's review the situation…
Read the report.	Let me explain…
Everybody else knows this.	How can I help you understand?

Prepare yourself and the receiver: use communication as an influencing tool

Influence is a key skill for managers, even with external stakeholders. You need the ability and willingness to share knowledge, multi-task, and put the client, internal or external, first.

 Tip

If you want to influence people, you will have to earn a reputation for openness, frankness and honesty. This is time-consuming, but the investment is more than rewarded by employee engagement and support from the managers above you.

Finally, failure to manage expectations can lead stakeholders to hold unrealistic expectations, followed by dissatisfaction and cynicism.

In terms of communication, you must also be a conceptualiser, developing plans to communicate and maintain relationships with various groups of stakeholders, in most cases the employees you manage. You will also need to be a counsellor: you should analyse the changing values, norms and issues of the company culture and in the markets, and discuss these with members of the organisation. You may counsel other members of the organisation, particularly top management, to make sure that they express the company's vision/mission, story and strategy accurately and honestly. You may also need to counsel them on the use of communication guidelines, policies and standards. At the same time, you're also a coach who helps the people you manage to communicate more effectively in order to serve the company strategy. Finally, you need to set the communication standard for the people who work for you, reminding them of its importance, checking messages and helping to formulate key messages.

Prepare yourself and the receiver: beware of filters

Filters are present in all of our communication systems. By definition, filters strain, separate, block, change, refine – they separate. Filters have a profound effect on how we encode and decode the messages we send and receive. People do what makes sense to them, based on what they understand and what they have experienced.

It is possible to make generalisations about typical filters through which you send and receive messages. Imagine drawing a map of the groups to which you belong. Figure 5.2 gives an example.

Figure 5.2 A group map

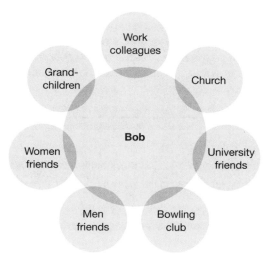

Each of the groups in Bob's life can be labelled according to the type of group they are. Within each one, Bob could make sub-groups as shown in Figure 5.3.

Figure 5.3 A sub-group map

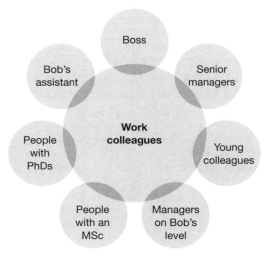

Bob could have made any number of groupings; this is just an example. The point is, no matter how Bob groups the people in social networks at work, these groups can represent filters through which Bob sends and receives information. This is not a map of Bob's prejudices, but Bob probably makes assumptions about people based on limited information and generalisations about the group. These generalisations may be about race and culture, but they could be about anything. Here's a generalisation I heard recently in a meeting with a group of marketing experts at a global bank: 'Computer engineers are anti-social geeks who usually know little about leadership and soft skills.'

 Tip

Most people have prejudices of one sort or another. Identifying prejudices may lead to them having a less negative influence on people's communication.

Common communication filters

Age
Life experience teaches us what is 'normal'. As we age our life experience changes our perspectives and how we view other people and the world. In companies, there is much talk about Baby Boomers, Generation X and Generation Y. Each group is described according to its age-related values and views.

Race and ethnicity
Racial and ethnic groups value some characteristics over others. Many of us think our way of doing things is 'natural', and other ways are wrong or weird. Some filters are more racial; others are more cultural. You should be aware of how your values may be filtering your messages.

Culture
Culture is like the default setting of a group. Cultural differences can have a strong impact on communication. Some cultures value the individual's contribution to the team over the cohesion of the team. In others, the individual subsumes himself or herself to the needs of the group: group harmony comes first. One culture puts the truth on the table; another believes it is best to let undiscussable topics remain unspoken. Five common pairs of culture-related traits have been identified:

1 **Individualism versus collectivism:** the degree to which we see ourselves as independent or part of a group.

2 **Tolerance for ambiguity:** the degree to which we tolerate ambiguity and uncertainty.

3 **Power relationships:** the degree to which we believe that access to power should be equally distributed.

4 **Masculinity/femininity:** the degree to which we value material things, power over others and assertiveness.

5 **High- versus low-context communication:** the degree to which we rely more on the explicit part of messages or more on the subtext.

▶

Gender

Gender combines culture, age, race, family life and experience to create each of us as an individual. It is one of the most common barriers to effective communication.

Women frequently use linguistic disclaimers, tag questions and 'I'm sorry' to maintain collegiality, connect and keep from sounding superior. Women often use non-verbal communication to signal encouragement.

Men's non-verbal signals tend to be less expressive. When women listen, their nodding means 'I hear you', not 'Yes'. Because women may often hope for collegiality, they often use language to soften hierarchical differences.

We are all individuals, but gender factors like the following must be taken into account:

1 *Hierarchy versus collegiality*: generally, women see the world of relationships in terms of collegiality, while men focus on hierarchy.

2 *The team*: Men tend to be comfortable on teams, letting the coach call the plays; women tend to see the coach as a mentor.

3 *Hiding information*: Men hide information and see it as fair play; women share information.

4 *Meet at the table or in the hall*: Women prepare for meetings by studying the material; men touch base with others to avoid surprises in the meeting. This may make meetings more like rituals, which often frustrates women.

5 *Success attribution*: Men often attribute success to their ability; women may attribute success to easy tasks and luck.

6 *Focus*: Men tend to do one thing at a time; women can juggle many projects at once. Men believe women bring superfluous points to meetings; women look at context and find that men focus too narrowly.

7 *Connecting*: Men often participate in 'male insult bonding greetings', which bewilders women. A woman's purpose for saying 'rude' things to another is not usually for bonding or banter. If this is misunderstood, it can be the cause for hurt feelings and insult. Non-verbally, women generally connect face-to-face; men often argue face-to-face.

▶

Language	Women tend to use more subtext than men. It's in the wiring of the brain. Women express themselves facially in ways that men often cannot detect (especially sadness). Women can identify the emotional states represented by facial expressions. Men who can identify a non-verbal expression are often unable to identify the associated emotion, especially sadness.
Body language	Many people put more credence in your non-verbal messages than in your words. A significant portion of a message is communicated through body language and tone of voice, not through the actual words.

Here are common gestures and expressions that cause inconsistent messages:

1 Speaking too loudly or too softly.
2 Smiling at the 'wrong places'.
3 Poor eye contact; no eye contact.
4 Leaning your head to one side.
5 Inappropriate humour, or no humour at all.

Assumptions and values	Our unexplored assumptions filter our messages. Our assumptions are often founded in the beliefs and values that rest at the 'core' of our beings. You will be a more effective communicator if your messages are aligned with your values. Knowing your values helps you recognise a communication filter. Being aware of your values also helps you check if your messages express your values. If people sense that your messages are not aligned with your values, they will perceive you as inauthentic and may stop listening.
Undiscussable topics	Sometimes assumptions are so significant that we do not dare mention them. These are 'undiscussable topics' – work-related problems that people hesitate to address. People talk about undiscussables frequently, but not out in the open because they are afraid to bring them up. Undiscussables make up much of the subtext in conversations. Common undiscussables are:

1 How people feel they are being treated by their bosses.
2 Whether their peers are doing a fair amount of work.
3 Unreasonable workloads and deadlines.
4 Tensions around diversity.
5 Tensions around working styles.
6 Compensation.

Step 2: Send your message

Send clear messages

We have been assuming that management communication is special because success depends on the degree to which you get your desired response – whatever that might be. Assuming this is true, the prize goes to managers who can send clear messages.

So what are the characteristics of a clear message? On the level of words, a clear message is not obscure. Unfortunately the world of management and business is, simply put, full of bullshit. Words so full of fuzz that nobody can tell you what they mean. All too often we get anything but the hard truth, honest language expressed with passion and a high degree of expressiveness. Straight talk is so rare that entire careers are built on it.

At General Electric's annual leadership meeting in Boca Raton, Florida, in January 1995, Jeff Immelt arrived late for dinner every evening and went to bed early, hoping to avoid a tough talk with his legendary boss, Jack Welch, about his poor performance. But on the last night of the meeting, he felt a hand on his shoulder just as he was rushing off. It was Welch:

Jeff,
I love you, and I know you can do better. But I'm going to take you out if you can't get it fixed.
Jack[1]

Messages can be verbal or non-verbal, but you need to make them, regardless of the mode of delivery, as clear as you can. What are the characteristics of a clear message? They are:

- clear (obviously)
- concise
- specific
- organised
- purposeful
- interesting.

Clear messages capture the right tone. Think of tone as the feel, sound, flavour, attitude or character of the words you use, combined with your voice. Your tone, whether in verbal or written messages, is created by the language you choose to present your message to your audience. Tone is also related to your persona, or the image you intend to portray to your audiences. Tone can range from sarcastic, to humorous, to serious, to questioning, to angry, to persuasive, to informative. Of course, you can choose and control your tone for various purposes and points you want to convey or emphasise.

Here are some questions to ask yourself about the tone of your messages:

- Do I use slang or colloquial language? Is the tone conversational?
- Do I use jargon and, therefore, direct the message toward a specialised audience?
- Do I use discipline-specific language, for example the language of IT or accounting? (Keep your use of jargon to a minimum.)
- What language do I use to create a certain tone? What is my tone? Formal or informal?
- How can I use tone to evoke a specific reaction or emotion from an audience?

When you're deciding on the purpose and goals of any communication, pay attention to the tone you want to create to achieve the most effective result. Your tone will affect how listeners or readers perceive your style and, in writing, your distinctive voice.

Messages can be 'high context' (with lots of subtext based on culture, credibility, experience, etc.) or low context (direct, with little subtext). Most people have

[1] 'The Fast Company Interview: Jeff Immelt', by John Byrne, *Fast Company*, 1 July 2005, www.fastcompany.com/magazine

preferences based on their filters, the other people involved in the communication and the type of message being conveyed. One member of your team may prefer email, another face-to-face communication.

Create simple, clear messages quickly

Effective messages are expressed in clear-cut, specific statements. A way to think about such messages is to make them SMART:[2]

- **S**pecific
- **M**easurable
- **A**ctionable
- **R**ealistic
- **T**ime stamped.

Simple language is just that: say what you need to say in as few words as possible. Effective spoken messages are delivered in a calm, non-critical tone of voice. No matter what your message, it will be received more openly if you make sure you are as 'objective' as you can be and that you remain composed.

Try to use 'we' statements instead of the 'you' form, which receivers may perceive as the verbal equivalent of finger-pointing. Nobody likes to feel accused! Try to express what you want in the other person's terms. This may look like an awful lot of effort to accommodate the other person's needs, but remember: you want results, and the receiver is the one you depend on to reach those results.

 Tip

1 Describe the situation and how it affects *you*. Give just the facts.
2 Say how you feel (sad, happy, angry, afraid, frustrated, etc.).
3 Say what you need. Describe the behaviour you need to see and a promise or commitment that it will happen.

Don't say: Don't you agree that we need to speed up the project?
Say: It would be a good idea to speed up the project.

---

[2] I would like to thank Susan Goldsworthy, previously Director Communication Tetra Pak AG, and now owner of Goldswolf Consulting, for sharing this tool with me.

Describe things factually. Make sure you can back up anything you say with facts that are clear and relevant.

> **Don't say:** He's the slowest web designer I've ever worked with.
> **Say:** He takes 30 per cent longer to complete his tasks than the other members of the web team.

When you are making an argument or building a case – much of the work of the manager – be sure to check your reasoning and evidence.

Send your message: test your reasoning

Ask yourself:

- Are the instances I cited typical?
- Have I accounted for negative instances?
- Have I addressed counter-arguments?
- Have I cited enough evidence to produce a valid conclusion?

Send your message: test your evidence

Ask yourself:

- What is the source of my evidence?
- Is my evidence accurate, current, relevant and sufficient?
- Have I properly evaluated the statistics?
- Have I cited valid authorities?
- Have I presented any inferences or opinions as fact?

Sending your message requires repetition. Conversations easily go off track. Have the courage to repeat your purpose several times in an interaction. If you send an important email, check for understanding and, if necessary, resend a modified version.

Here are some examples of typical management messages that don't meet the 'clarity' tests. After each one is a revised version (there is no one correct version).

> **Original:** I need the quarterly budget breakdowns as soon as possible.
> **Revised:** Please email me the report by 10:00 tomorrow.
> **Original:** A new HR policy has been drafted to cover employee attendance issues.
> **Revised:** Dr Quinsy in HR has written a new policy to cover attendance and lateness; it is effective immediately.

Use the following tips to clarify your message.

1 In one sentence, summarise your main point (not your purpose, but your actual point). Say it out loud. To check clarity, record it on your smartphone and play it back. It is essential that you capture this point in one sentence.

2 Express why you are trying to convey this message. This is your purpose (which should relate to getting a particular response from a particular audience).

3 List the reasons why someone should be interested in your message. Think of the reasons why they may not be. Ask yourself:

- How can I appeal to the self-interests of the audience?
- How can I express my message in terms of benefits for them (so-called 'audience benefits')?
- Have you made it clear why they should be interested? In other words, have you answered the 'So what' question?

4 Now express your message in a logical manner. Most messages in management ultimately answer the questions 'how, what, when and why'. Whatever organising principle you choose, be sure that your reader or listener will be able to follow you:

- past to future
- left to right
- large to small
- main idea with three sub-points: think of your message in the shape of a pyramid: main point at the top, with three main 'blocks' supporting it afterwards.
- if you are selling an idea or making a recommendation, consider organising your message as follows:

  the problem → the cause of the problem → your solution to the problem → why your solution is better than all other possible solutions.

5 If you are building an argument, decide whether to present just your side, or also possible refutations, which you can then debunk. Also decide, depending on the bias of your audience (positive, neutral or negative), whether you want to start with your main point or argument and then support it, or whether you want to take a softer approach – supporting arguments first, leading to your

main point. The more hostile your audience, the more likely you will need to build a softer, indirect argument.

6 To make your message specific, be sure to communicate which things, what items, whose ideas, where and when something happened, and how many people were involved.

7 To make sure you capture the interest of the reader or listener, you need to make sure your message is relevant. So be sure to state why this message should be of interest to the audience. Now that you know something about the filters that can block communication, think about the ones that your audience may use. Think about their temperament, interests, culture and communication preferences.

8 Consider the subtext. Ask yourself:

- What feeling do I want to convey?
- Do I want or need to be polite, clever, credible, firm, etc.? This will help you get the tone right.
- Reread what you have written or, for a presentation or public speaking event, practise your main points. Rehearse. In speaking, never underestimate the power of preparation. In writing, never underestimate the power of editing. Effective writing is effective editing.

9 Finally, always ask:

- How could this go wrong?
- What are the possible negative reactions?
- How might I be misunderstood?
- What may get in the way of my audience receiving my intended message?

Sending your message in a presentation

Presentations have become ubiquitous in organisations. There are thousands of books and websites devoted to slide presentations. In spite of this, we all still sit through hours and hours of mind-numbing, energy-sucking, lifeless, confusing, and seemingly pointless slide presentations.

What can you do about this problem immediately? First, avoid the common mistakes:

- **Don't conceive of your presentation as an act of explanation or clarification.** Countless managers stiffly click through their slides, practically reading out loud from a script. Your presentation is an act of persuasion.

- **Don't see your presentation as a performance.** The aim of any presentation is to connect with your listeners. It's a conversation. You want to show empathy, engage, to keep them listening to you, spark their curiosity.

- **Stop worrying about mechanics.** Much has been made of various presentation techniques: standing in front of the podium, scanning the room, making eye contact, not gesticulating wildly with your hands, asking rhetorical questions. If you connect with the audience, most of these concerns will take care of themselves.

- **Ignore the old myth that effective presentations are really about body language.** Trainers and experts often tell people about the research that 'proves' that only a tiny percentage of a successful presentation comes from content, while the majority of what the audience perceives and understands results from the presenter's body language. You will often hear the same claim about communication in general. If the content is dull, then of course people will remember the speaker's voice and body language. Visit the website www.TED.com and you can watch amazingly engaging talks by people who have something fascinating to say, but who say it 'badly' (at least according to much of the advice you get from presentation experts). Take look at Malcolm Gladwell on www.TED.com. Gladwell, it seems, never has anything dull to say. His content is unendingly interesting. And yet, as a presenter he is painfully shy. Listeners may comment on his shyness, but you can be sure they remember his comments about 'outliers' or 'success'.

- **Don't ever give a presentation if you can't summarise the main point and purpose in a sentence or two.** When you don't plan your presentation well, you will have no identifiable goal. You'll wander. And so will your audience. Decide what type of presentation you want to deliver and what the goal should be. Analyse your audience and plan the message to move the audience from where they are today to the desired goal. Without a clear message, you'll waste the audience's time.

- **Make sure the audience can see what's on the screen.** If the audience can't see what is on the screen, they certainly won't be getting the message.

- For text, **you should build bullet points that take the audience step by step through a logical progression of ideas.** Your graphs and tables should give visual *life* to concepts and diagrams that break down and illustrate complex ideas.

- **Stay away from most of the whizz-bang features in presentation software.** Don't distract your audience with flying and rotating and dissolving objects. Stick to relevant images (photographs are good) and simple words and phrases. Use lots of white space. If the audience can't make sense of your slide in two seconds, it's too complex. If your company culture demands that you hand out slides, create a second version with your notes on the notes pages, or with more detailed text. **A good rule of thumb is: the slide should have no value to the audience without you. You are the presentation, not your slides.** If watching your slides drains your audience's energy, you need to improve them.

- **Practice, practice, practice:** If you can't give your presentation without your slides and presentation software, you're in trouble. The slides should complement your talk, not be your talk. Make sure you finish early, to give time for questions and answers. Early means, for example, that in an hour, you devote at least 15 minutes to Q&As. When you move from slide to slide, or make a transition from point to point, blank out the screen.

Prepare	*Define your purpose*	Why am I giving this presentation?
		What do I want to achieve?
		What do I want the audience to *do* afterwards?
	Analyse your audience	What do I want them to think, believe or feel?
		Are they positive, neutral or negatively biased toward me and my subject?
		Who are the decision makers?
		How interested are they in the theme?
		What will they win or lose if they take my advice?
		Why might they reject my ideas?
		What are the three most difficult questions the audience might ask?
	Scope your presentation	Can I achieve my purpose in the time I have?
		If I had only half the time, what would I say?
		If I had only three minutes, what would I say?
	Choose the media	Are there effective alternatives to presentation software? Discussion, handouts, flipcharts.
		How can I use the flipchart in places?
		Where can I turn the beamer off?
Design	*Articulate the message*	How would I summarise my presentation in 30 seconds? One minute? Three minutes?
		Why do I really need more time than that?
		Ask: 'What am I really trying to say, in a nutshell?'
		How would I convey the same material, without presentation software?

▶

	Structure the content	Introduction: goal, meaning, preview **Main section:** one key message with three supporting points. I need to answer what I think the audience's three main questions will be, in the order I think they would ask them. Imagine an hour-long presentation as 5–7 slides. How will this change my presentation? **Closing:** summary of main points, recommendations, action programme, next steps.
	Create a storyboard	Sketch your main slides on Post-it notes. This manual work will help you 'see' your slides and your logic better. Audience questions are best answered with the following: What? Text, images, models Where? Maps, plans Who? Organisation chart, photos When? Calendar, Gantt charts How? Diagrams How much? Simple tables and diagrams Why? Text Determine the best order: every slide must have a message, either stated or implied. Check the logic in the 'outline' or 'light table' view. You must have a 'red thread' running through the presentation. Make sure that your slides 'need you'. The audience should never be reading your slides instead of listening to you.
Delivery	*First practice*	Get familiar with your argument and slides. Make notes (only if absolutely necessary). Practise with the recording option on your smartphone – video and audio!
	Second practice	Practise with an empathetic colleague. Practise answering the most likely audience questions, especially negative or hostile ones. Watch a video of your own performance.

Prepare the venue	Take full responsibility for the room and the technical support.
	Take 'ownership' of the room. Walk around. Get to see the room from the perspective of your audience.
	Practise your opening and get to know the beamer and pointer equipment.
	If you plan to use a flipchart, consider bringing extra-thick markers for making large, simple diagrams. This takes some practice but can be far more compelling for the audience than watching slides.
Tips from the pros	Breathe, breathe, breathe.
	Make eye contact.
	Open yourself to the audience.
	Speak in a natural voice (find your natural pitch).
	Use the full range of your voice.
	Do not worry about your hands – if you are natural, comfortable, and want to reach out to the audience, your hands will be fine. If in doubt, reach your hands out toward the audience and keep them between your hips and shoulders.
	Find your passion for the material and bring that passion and energy into your presentation.
	Stand next to the screen and don't look back at it too often.
	Join the audience, if appropriate.
	Balance your weight on both feet, feel the floor.
Using slides	Make transitions to the next slide *before* you show it.
	Show the slide – explain it – take it away.
	Use the flipchart to 'draw' your table, graph or simple image.
Dealing with questions	Make eye contact.
	Listen, listen, listen.
	Pause before you answer (count to three).
	Answer the question asked, not more or less.
	Refer back to your presentation.

Send your message in a story

In recent years, there has been much talk about the powers of storytelling as a managerial communication tool. Strategic storytelling is the telling of stories to achieve a desired communication purpose. From 2005 to 2007, I interviewed more than 50 senior executives in 30 large international companies to explore their views of storytelling as a managerial communication tool. The senior executives described their companies as communication contexts where logical argument, credibility from functional expertise and logical persuasion are paramount and where managers need to wear 'corporate armour' to get on with their careers. Influence ('persuading people to act') was seen as a key management tool. But gaining influence was seen as difficult in large, widely dispersed and highly networked organisations, where managers may need to persuade people over whom they have no official power.

Managers saw many advantages and risks in strategic storytelling. Different cultures have different degrees of acceptance of the idea of managers using stories. Storytelling is easy to do badly, and hard to get right, requiring time and effort that often offer only marginal returns. Managers who tell stories face performance risks: a loss of personal and professional credibility, a failure to tell a story that is relevant to the audience, organisational resistance to storytelling and the fear of anti- or counter-stories.

Nevertheless, strategic storytelling was seen as a potentially valuable communication tool in many contexts, especially as a complement to other, more widely used communication vehicles. The emotional power of storytelling was seen as one of its highest values.

 Tip

In certain situations, a short, focused story can achieve communication goals more effectively than conventional communication modes like direct and indirect argument.

Stories hold influence potential. A well-told, 'authentic' story can engage audience members emotionally, and this engagement can build the manager's credibility. Increased credibility means more influence. And better rapport.

Well-chosen stories are powerful ways to build metaphors, spark visualisation, engage the imagination, and make abstract information more concrete. They can generate action, make pedagogical points, enable indirect messaging, boost persuasive power and entertain. But these communication purposes are subjugated to the overarching goal of gaining and wielding influence.

You can learn to use this powerful tool, so long as you accept some basic 'rules'.

Tip

- **A strategic story needs a clear, well-articulated purpose.** The teller needs to be invested personally in the story, should believe it and be passionate about it.
- **The teller has to be prepared, but not overly prepared.** Practice is vital. Simple, clear storytelling instructions, 'safe' training, a guidebook or framework, and multi-media examples of effective and ineffective storytelling can help you learn strategic storytelling.
- **A good story touches people in some way.** It should best be drawn from the world of the company, culled from personal experience of the teller or audience. A good story involves the audience, makes them interact with the teller and the story, even if it is only in their thoughts. It is not the teller who tells the story; it is the listener, the audience.
- **A good story creates vivid images.** When you tell a story, you create images for your listeners. They may not see the same images you see and imagine, but that is the exciting part of storytelling. As the story unfolds, you want them to imagine their own images and experiences. This is the part that makes interaction so important. If our stories help the listener to think of his or her own stories, we have succeeded in igniting a storytelling spark.
- **A good story has a sense of truth.** It resonates with some basic universal aspects of being human. It doesn't have to be profound, but a good story should move the listeners, make them laugh, think, and ponder it afterwards. Stories must tap into the emotions, be extremely short, build the teller's credibility, have a built-in business or management lesson and be highly relevant to the audience in the given context.
- **Strategic stories do not need a traditional plot.** They need a loose structure that orders events and has at least one character (which may be the 'the company') experiencing challenges and acting on them. Professional storytellers often talk about the 'bones' of a story. This is its basic outline or skeleton. If the skeletal structure is strong, chances are you have a good story.

Good places to use stories are to open presentations, to serve as examples during presentations, in public speeches, and in meetings to make a point. One CEO I interviewed was running a major change programme at a liquid food company. He settled on the story of how Tiger Woods, at the height of his early success, decided to rework his swing. This re-engineering took Woods many months, and caused him to slip in the golf rankings. And yet he believed in his vision of a better swing. Ultimately, he succeeded. The CEO used this story as a metaphor throughout the company's change programme.

Tell your story in a logical manner. Organise it past to future, left to right, large to small, idea to sub-points, using a consistent progression to help the listener or reader follow you. One effective way is to follow these steps.

 Tips

1 **Describe a problem or challenge you or you company faced.**
2 **Describe the cause of the problem.**
3 **Describe up to five actions you took to resolve the problem, but failed.**
4 **Describe the action you took that finally solved the problem.**
5 **Describe the net benefits of your action.**
6 **Describe the lesson learned and how it can be applied to the future.**

A good story needs conflict and resolution. Stories are made up of people, places and happenings. Strong management stories have a well-defined main character – a manager and/or a company – that runs into some kind of trouble. Something blocks the main character: another person, another company, market forces, operational breakdowns or even the main character. The character's actions lead to personal growth and change – possibly an 'aha!' – and finally, some sort of redemption. Believable action keeps the audience entranced as the story moves from beginning to middle to end. They want to know what's going to happen. Once they find out, they need to see how the story is relevant to their situation and how the lesson learned is relevant to their business challenges.

Here's another, more general, way to build a story.

Building a story

1 Think of a point you want to illustrate with a story. Build a simple scaffold of three main events.
2 Why is this message valuable for this audience? Why is a story the best way to convey the message? How will they relate to the story?
3 Is your company a good place to tell a story? Will people be open to it? Is there any risk to your credibility?
4 What feelings do you have about it, and how will you infuse them into your story? What you do want the audience to do after they hear it?
5 What's your purpose in telling the story?

6   What tone do you want to use? Energetic, loud, with lots of movement or more subdued? Will you whisper or project?
7   What details should you include to make it credible?
8   How will you find time to rehearse? Never tell a story without rehearsing it. I suggest ten practice sessions. Best if you record it once. And practise it once in a room the same size as the planned venue. Tell it to people and get their reactions. Ironically, the more you practise your story (or presentation for that matter), the more natural you will appear. Never try to memorise your story word for word. Rote memory is a recipe for disaster: you will come off as wooden and stiff.

Send your message assertively

Being assertive is not just a matter of phrasing clear messages. Being assertive means being passionate when you discuss a topic that matters to you, not backing down too quickly from your opinion, but also considering others' feelings without letting go of your own. Assertiveness is not about *what* you are saying; it is about *how* you are saying it. No matter what you are trying to say, it is always possible to express yourself assertively.

Many managers have difficulties being assertive in a constructive way. They are either too passive or overly aggressive. Excessively passive managers do not express their preferences or ask to have their needs met. Managers who are excessively aggressive push others away and wind up disconnected, which fosters poor performance.

The passive–aggressive continuum, or scale, is a way to think about how assertive you are (see Figure 5.4). You want to be in the middle, not at the less effective ends of the continuum.

Figure 5.4 The passive–aggressive continuum

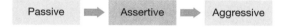

A manager at the passive end places too little value on his or her needs, and too much on the needs and rights of the people around him. Passive managers often try to meet the needs of the other person. They don't talk, they listen. But they only listen. An example might be a new manager promoted from the ranks of colleagues in a group, who suddenly finds herself unable to assert her needs over the needs of her ex-colleagues.

Aggressive managers don't consider the rights and needs of the people around them. Their overarching goal is meeting their own needs, even at the expense of others. They don't listen, they talk. They dominate and bully to get their way. There is no shortage of caricatures of such managers. In recent years, the heads of global investment banks have been portrayed – fairly or unfairly – as aggressive.

The assertive manager places equal value on the needs and rights of the self and the needs and rights of others. When you are being assertive, your goal is reciprocity and balance. You try to treat both yourself and your company colleagues with respect.

Most of us move back and forth on the assertiveness continuum. You may be passive in one situation and then fly into a rage over some seemingly minor matter; then, in remorse, sink back into passivity and start the cycle again. Alternatively, you may be aggressive for a time, and then swing to passivity. Another common pattern is to be 'passive-aggressive'. The passive-aggressive manager appears to be passive but is actually aggressive. For example, say your boss asks you for a 'favour' that you consider excessive and unreasonable. You feel angry at your boss and you want to say 'no'. If you were to handle this situation passive-aggressively, you would say 'yes' and then not follow through. You would forget, or bungle the favour somehow, or do it too late. On the surface you would seem affable and willing, but in fact you would be expressing anger at the boss by not following through with the request.

A serious negative consequence of being passive is poor communication. You don't ask for what you want or get what you need; your rights get trampled regularly (or so it feels); and you have to cope with a growing sense of resentment that boils below the surface. Common symptoms are headaches, anxiety, depression, inner conflict, stress and insomnia. These are likely to limit your ability to get things done.

A negative consequence of aggression is the emotional cost. You push colleagues away, even the ones you depend on most. After a while your superiors, colleagues and employees ignore you or they retaliate. You may lose your job, get into arguments or fights, cause colleagues to dislike socialising with you, or otherwise pay for being a bully. And your communication will suffer, because you lose power, credibility, trust and rapport.

To improve your assertiveness skills, ask yourself what style you use naturally, and also ask how your style may look to people who use another more or less assertive style. Complete this self-test:

Statement	Self-rating			
	Never	Sometimes	Often	Always
I am honest with myself about my feelings and needs.				
I tell others what I feel.				
I am open and honest in my evaluations of my employees' performances.				
When I think someone is treating me unfairly, I say so.				
If someone pressures me to do something I don't want to do, I refuse.				
When I disagree with someone, I say so in a way they understand.				
When someone is unfair, I point it out.				
If I think there's a problem in a working relationship, I tell the other person.				
I ask for help when I need it.				
If someone asks me for a favour I think is inconvenient, I say so.				
I tell employees the ways I rely on them, what I expect from them and why.				

Practise being less passive or less aggressive until you know exactly how assertively you want to handle yourself in every management scenario that is likely to come up. Know how you will communicate if the other person responds well, and also how you will communicate if they respond badly. The way the other person responds is *not* the important thing. Most important is that you reach your goals and handle yourself well.

Here are some tips for finding an effective balance between passivity and aggression.

Tips

1 **Respect yourself and the other person equally.** After every important conversation, ask yourself: Did I maintain my self-respect? Did I respect the
   other person?

2 **Ask for what you need.** State your preferences.

3 **Assert your rights, but don't be hurtful.**

4 **Define your goal.** What are you trying to accomplish? Your overarching
   goal is always to behave assertively – to respect both yourself and the other
   person equally. Changing the other person is not one of your goals. They
   may or may not change; that is outside your control. Judge the success of
   an assertiveness exercise by how well you have behaved.

5 **Choose an appropriate setting.** Choose a time and place that will most help
   you achieve your assertiveness goals. Most managers have enough positional
   power to be able to dictate the venue of a meeting. Most people prefer quiet,
   privacy and peace for a conversation that requires assertiveness.

6 **If possible, pick a time when the other person is calm.** Try your best to
   pick a time when the other person is likely to be receptive to what you have
   to say.

7 **Stay calm.** Don't confuse assertiveness with anger. Express your feelings,
   but do not lose your temper, yell, dominate the other person physically, or
   call the person names. If you feel you are going to lose control, leave the
   meeting until you have regained control.

8 **Use assertive body language.** Stand or sit up straight, look the other person
   in the eye (unless the other person's culture will take it as an offence) and
   speak in a clear and audible voice.

9 **Be as brief and as clear as possible.** The more brief and clear you are, the
   more powerful your message will be.

10 **Talk about your feelings, not about some objective 'rightness'.** Don't
   preach to the other person about right and wrong. Speak in a personal way.
   Use 'I feel' statements, like: 'I feel angry that you…'; 'I feel uncomfortable
   when you…'; 'I don't like it when you…'.

11 **Do not get defensive.** Do not over-justify your feelings. Do not list all the
   reasons why you are speaking. Your feelings are enough justification. You
   do not need to expand in this case.

12 **Request specific, verifiable behavioural change.** Tell the person exactly what you want them to do to correct the situation. Be specific and concrete. Criticise the behaviour, not the person. Say: 'I don't like it when you come late to meetings,' not, 'You are chaotic.' Say, 'Please start arriving on time,' not, 'Stop being so absent-minded.'

13 **When you want to say something negative, start and end with positives.** Use positives that are true; don't make up positives.

14 **If the other person protests, simply keep restating your position.** Stay on track and stay true to your goal. Don't get lost in arguments the other person raises. Don't go off on tangents. Don't retreat because you have trouble tolerating the other person's anger. No matter what the other person says, just calmly and succinctly keep repeating your point.

Step 3: Check for understanding

A common communication myth among managers is that sending a message is like sending a package. You write up your simple, clear message, run the spell check and hit 'SEND'. You give your speech, make your presentation – your work is done. Many managers are hyper-aware of the first two steps in communication. Some skip the preparation part. Effective communication requires that you verify with your receiver that they have received your message and understood it as you intended. This important step is all about listening actively. Active listening requires asking questions and paraphrasing:

● What do you think of what I just said?
● Let's recap what we've said so far, or here's what we've said or agree so far.
● Tell me your views or thoughts.
● Let's make sure we're on the same page. Tell me what you heard.
● Does this make sense?
● Do you have any questions? Concerns? Suggestions?

Some people believe that active listening involves concentrating hard on what someone is saying, straining to memorise it, but doing this passively. Effective listening is active: it goes beyond mere 'storing' other people's words. I had a colleague who told me that he always took detailed notes in meetings with prospective clients so they would think he was listening. But his method wasn't effective listening because he failed to ask his conversation partners open questions to demonstrate that he was not only hearing their words, but 'listening' to their wishes and concerns.

Active listening is hard and time-consuming. It isn't about giving answers, stating directions or taking control of a conversation. It requires proof of understanding and respect, and nearly 100 per cent of your attention. Skilled listeners care about the people they are listening to. If you listen to employees and other important stakeholders you will 'hear' the most important messages of all: the subtext and non-verbal messages.

Do you exhibit any of the common behaviours of 'poor listeners' listed below?

Poor listeners	Skilled listeners
Glance at watch, tap foot, drum fingers	Make eye contact, use nodding, say words of encouragement
Finish people's sentences, make assumptions	Paraphrase speaker's words, clarify, summarise
Interrupt, correct the speaker	Calmly state views as appropriate
Focus on delivery or mannerisms	Focus on content
Shut down group participation	Encourage group participation
React emotionally	Not defensive; not over-emotional
Ignore non-verbal cues	Attend to non-verbal cues
Get caught up with emotions	Take time out when needed
Dramatise reactions or feelings	Maintain open posture and expression
Try to control others' feelings	Respect others' feelings
Talk more than they listen	Listen more than they talk

Many managers are extremely skilled at 'probing' or questioning (like in-depth interviews), but they are less effective at reflecting or summarising. To improve your listening skills, practise paraphrasing or making reflecting statements to summarise the content and feelings of what someone else has said to you. Don't try to move the conversation along. Try to confirm what has already been said, or agreed.

Paraphrasing appears to be so simple that many managers think it isn't important. But if you don't do it naturally, or genuinely, it comes off feeling to others like a skill you learned in a communication workshop. Remember: a parrot in front of a bar in Key West, Florida can repeat back simple sentences. Paraphrasing in routine management conversations isn't 'parrot-phrasing'. You need to capture speaker content and intent, feelings and nuanced subtleties of language, non-verbal cues and the subtext (for example, enthusiasm or sarcasm, disappointment or hope).

You don't need to summarise every sentence in a conversation. Do it maybe twice in a five-minute conversation to show the speaker you are 'with them'.

Effective paraphrasing and questioning can keep people who ramble on track.

Build rapport

Management depends on productive relationships. Yet these relationships today often span cultures, classes, disciplines and business functions. You need to be polite and respectful, and respect cultural differences, and yet not be evasive, boring or irrelevant. Building rapport with people from different cultures, age groups, education levels and perspectives is hard work. You have to communicate with people who are essentially alien to you, find ways to talk to them directly, with an understanding of their perspectives and background. And when misunderstandings crop up, you need to detect them fast and handle them effectively. This means listening actively and making connections.

When you've got rapport with someone, you understand each other's feelings or ideas. Rapport involves understanding one another as well as feeling compassion or empathy for the other's situation. It is built on the verbal and the non-verbal level. Here are a few ways to build rapport quickly.

Building rapport

- **Greet others.**
- **Look people in the eye.**
- **Give the person your full attention.**
- **Listen carefully and avoid interrupting.**
- **Be sincere and genuine.** Make only promises you can keep.
- **Use an appropriate sense of humour.** Be sensitive to filters, assumptions and different values.
- **Use encouragement consciously.** Comment on people's work, their helping someone, favours they've done, taking over a project task when a colleague was out of the office – anything that made a contribution to the success of the company. Never compliment someone for something inherently untrue, superficial or false.
- **Use expressive and receptive body language.** This non-verbal aspect of building rapport literally involves mirroring how your communication partner sits, stands and uses the body. Mirroring is the art of making the other person feel comfortable by matching his or her style of communication. It includes matching vocal volume and speed, and body language, like leaning forward or backward when your communication partner leans forward or backward.

- **Try to match the other person's rate of speech.** If your conversation partner speaks quietly, speak more quietly yourself. Converse with a shouter, not by shouting back, but by raising the volume of your voice a few decibels. If you are talking with a highly energetic person who bubbles with energy and gesticulates wildly, try to mirror this 'loudness'. Be aware of the so-called interruption gaps in your conversations. An interruption gap is the amount of silence after asking a question or making a statement.
- **Control your voice.** Voice volume is how loud you are. Make sure you project, but don't yell. Aim for your 'middle' pitch, where you are comfortable speaking. Speaking too fast implies hurry and disinterest; speaking too slowly implies you're slow, even slow-minded and perhaps too cautious.
- **Watch your distance.** The more comfortable we are with people, the closer we can be to them. Intimate distance is closest; public distance is farthest away. Different cultures have different norms for intimate and public distance. In the Anglo-Saxon world, a common distance for two people in a work situation is around two feet apart.

Positive and negative feedback

Giving and receiving feedback is a tricky business. Finding the right words for negative feedback can be difficult. If you overdo it, positive feedback can sound hollow and disingenuous.

Let's start with positive feedback – the easier one. Positive feedback takes only a few seconds and little effort. And it's a top motivator. It's so easy you have to wonder why more managers don't do it. Many managers who are perceived as effective communicators plan at least once a day to give positive feedback to someone who works for them.

With positive feedback, you need to distinguish between praise and flattery. If you flatter someone, your comments may focus on what someone has no control over and did nothing to earn. Praise focuses on commendable character, performance or behaviour. Train yourself to give regular praise for good, measurable performance. Consider praising your superiors. Some managers take the view that if they don't say anything, their employees will assume the silence means they're doing a good job. Unfortunately, the employee may take the silence as veiled criticism, or unspoken displeasure.

If giving praise makes you uncomfortable, try giving praise when you don't want anything in particular. To lessen an awkward moment when your compliment makes someone self-conscious, simply follow it with a question. For example, 'Good job handling that customer complaint. Have you worked with her before?' The other person can focus on answering your question.

You can also tell another staff member what a fine job a third person is doing. Such an intermediary passes on the comment and boosts the morale of the praised person because it is even more believable when delivered as 'fact' by a colleague. Make sure, however, that you don't put the intermediary in an awkward position, or make them wonder why they didn't get the praise.

Sooner or later, every manager has to give negative feedback. Before you give any criticism, ask yourself why you need to give negative feedback, and make sure it is in the best interests of the company and person. Sometimes you will have to choose: you will have to side with the company, but you can, nevertheless, find ways to make the criticism a productive experience for the employee. Focus your criticism on the fact that it is a chance for the employee to improve. Here are some behaviours to avoid.

 Tips

Here are some to avoid:

- **Not knowing the facts of the case: you need concrete examples.**
- **Engaging in the same behaviour yourself.**
- **Using trapping questions: 'Do you want our guests to feel happy with our service?' Such questions involve assumptions that may not be accurate.**
- **Giving negative feedback in public.**
- **Using comments that are too general: 'Sometimes your tone is too gruff.'**
- **Comparing people: 'You really need to learn to deal with guests like Mary does. She's always calm and friendly.'**

Receiving negative feedback

Sooner or later, your boss, or someone above you in the organisational hierarchy is going to give you negative feedback. Negative feedback can stop you in your tracks. You start to question what you're doing, and why. Your negative self-talk increases. You criticise others. To stop this negative doom loop, always filter negative feedback. Don't lose your motivation and proper peace of mind. Don't immediately deny anything. Don't go on the counterattack. Don't try to rationalise your behaviour. At some point, it made sense to you! Don't accept the criticism superficially. 'Sure, sure, you're right, I'll get to that.' Don't assume that negative criticism is meant to tear you down or destroy you. Never pretend that 'It's no big deal.' Unhappy customers, for example, can make your life a misery. Don't harp on about it.

What can you do to benefit from negative feedback without being paralysed, demotivated or made unproductive by it?

Successful negative feedback

A more successful 'negative' feedback session would include such tactics as:

- **Separate fact from opinion.**
- **Anticipate reactions:** give the employee time to consider what you're saying and respond. Be prepared to schedule a follow-up meeting.
- **Start the conversation with a question:** 'How did you feel about your conversation with Dr Rao?'
- **Give feedback on one thing at a time:** choose one instance of the person's inappropriate tone of voice or interrupting a guest.
- **Focus on problem solving:** 'What could you have said to keep John from losing his temper and complaining to me?'
- **Be specific.** Explain why the employee's behaviour is a problem. Give examples.
- **Acknowledge the employee's feelings and point of view.** Perhaps she is under a great deal of stress and meeting your expectations and the guests' is getting harder and harder.
- **Include credit as well as criticism.** Tell the employee what she does well.
- **Focus on behaviour, not on the person.** Try using adverbs that modify actions ('You talked gruffly with the people from the bank, and they complained about it to me'), not adjectives that modify characteristics ('You're a gruff person, Anne, and you need to change.').
- **Foster change of behaviour with praise.** 'I saw you did a very good job dealing with Mr and Mrs Kline when they complained that the red wine in their room was too cold.'
- **Focus on the future.** Paint a picture of the benefits to the employee if he changes his behaviour.
- **End the session with encouragement.** 'You're one of our best employees, and I look forward to you making your good performance even better.'

Tips

- **Actively invite negative feedback**, especially when you're going to hear it anyway. Determine who you will listen to: superiors, colleagues, customers, stakeholders, etc. Accept your imperfections. Accept the imperfections of others. You're going to trip up once in a while. The trick is to bounce back fast.

- **Avoid defensive reactions.** Determine how useful the feedback is. Can I learn from it? Could I improve from it? What's the lesson? Don't muster a defence when no defence is needed. Negative feedback is difficult to digest if it contains at least some small truth. Keep your pride out of it. Give yourself some time before you react. Take a breather.

- **Listen to the entire message before you respond.** Take notes if necessary.

- **Ask questions** to get specific examples (if not given) and to buy time to overcome defensive feelings.

- **Be willing to accept responsibility.** But keep your strengths in mind.

- **Be sensitive to the speaker's feelings and point of view.** Ask how they would have handled the situation.

- **Summarise or paraphrase** what the other person said and clarify any misunderstandings.

- **Assess the criticism.** What is the source? What are the critic's motivations? Is it valid? Is it important? Criticism from a client is almost always important, but may not be valid. Beware of the dangerous 'half-truth'. Look at the entire statement, not just the individual points. Ask what your critic's hidden agenda may be. Consider the subtext.

Communicating in conflict

Some conflicts arise or escalate merely because of how we are handling our communication. When you face a conflict, you're unlikely to be an effective communicator. To be an effective communicator in conflict situations, pay attention to the details of language and follow a few simple guidelines.

> ## Guidelines for effective communications in conflict
>
> - Use 'I' messages and positive intent; check assumptions.
> - Separate the person from the message: focus on behaviour, not personality.
> - Listen actively.
> - Structure the conflict conversation by stating your intention, which is to discuss the issue, improve the situation and usually build on something in the past, rather than characterising your view as a negation of the other person's. Here's an example:
>   - I want to talk about your behaviour and/or comments. Offer an apology if appropriate.
>   - I acknowledge your view.
>   - Your behaviour affects my work or me in this way.
>   - I want (this) to happen.
>   - Let's see if we can do some things differently that will iron out our differences. Express a commitment to mutual gain.
> - Try to turn a disagreement into dialogue by committing to understand each other. End the conversation with a working agreement in which you clarify your expectations.

Most conflict situations, like the one above, require that you deal with emotions and feelings you encounter before you can get to resolution. A powerful tool here is detached responsibility. Detached responsibility may be new to you and the people you communicate with at work. It's the same attitude that a mediator cultivates during a tense mediation or negotiation. Detached responsibility involves using that same mindset in your own conflict situations. The components of detached responsibility are:

- **Desire:** to collaboratively achieve a mutually beneficial outcome.
- **Discipline:** to address unpleasant or uncomfortable situations.
- **Dedication:** to allow the process time to work.

Dealing with hot heads

Sometimes managers have to deal with people who blow up regularly because it gets them results. Communicating with them can be taxing. One tactic is to seek more information, ask questions, try to 'get to the bottom' of the anger. This way you catch the angry person off-guard and open a new avenue for dialogue. Let the angry person save face. Validate their feelings. Try asking: 'Is there anything else? I'd like to hear everything you have to say.' Use an even, non-critical tone of voice.

If the person shows no signs of calming down, 'self-preservation' tactics may be necessary. Here are tips for handling a really angry person.

 Tips

- **Deal with the person now, or as soon as possible.**
- **Move to a private location.**
- **Respond to emotions first.**
  - **Acknowledge feelings, then paraphrase to ensure you understood the issue.**
  - **'I know we both have strong opinions about this. I want to understand your view.'**
- **Let them vent.**
  - **Don't interrupt.**
  - **Probe for more.**
- **Use 'self-preservation' tactics if necessary.**
  - **Disrupting questions: 'When did you begin thinking that…';**
  - **Computer mode: Avoid 'I' or 'you' statements and use neutral statements instead. Example: 'Many people think that…'. 'That's an interesting viewpoint…'.**
- **Find agreement about something. For example: 'I think we agree that we don't want this issue to affect other projects we're working on.'**

What if none of this works? Try this:

 Tips

- **Use perception checking: confirm the behaviour you believe was confrontational.**
- **Allow time for reflection and silence. Breathe. Pause.**
  - **Your silence shows acceptance, promotes a safe environment, and encourages a less defensive reaction.**
  - **Some people need more time to reflect and process information.**

Hidden agendas

Another communication conflict is dealing with hidden agendas. A hidden agenda is simply a secret or hidden motive for something. Your boss promotes you, not because he thinks you're doing a great job, but because he thinks your mediocrity will make him look good. Your manager sends you to an important client meeting, not because he trusts you, but because he knows the client is angry and he doesn't want to face the client's wrath. In these cases, you are being set up to fail.

How do you know if the root of the conflict is a hidden agenda? How can you recognise a hidden agenda? Here are some clues:

- Information isn't shared.
- Decisions are delayed.
- Rumours are rampant.
- One or the other party is unable to focus on the issue at hand.
- The conflict escalates.
- Agreements aren't carried out.

Try adopting these strategies to uncover the hidden agendas that may be disrupting your communication processes.

- Refuse to talk about an issue unless the people directly involved are included.
- Refuse to listen to, speculate about or spread rumours.
- Ask direct questions: 'Do you disagree with the decision?'
- Probe. For example, 'I'm getting lots of positive response for my new proposal, but no one shows up when I call a meeting to discuss it further. Can I have a few minutes with you to talk about your feelings about this project?'
- Break the conflict into sub-issues to expose specific concerns.
- Attempt to discover the concerns behind the issues by clarifying facts and perceptions:
  - Find out what happened.
  - Get clear on the specifics.
  - Focus on concerns.
  - Determine what's been concluded about what happened.
  - Separate conclusions from facts.
  - Identify facts that support opinions.

Prepare a personal strategic communication action plan

Successful personal communication requires a long-term perspective, honesty about your communication strengths and weaknesses, planning and preparation for each communication. We have focused on the three-step communication model and some self-analysis of your skills. Now you need to start thinking long-term, to see the entire constellation of your communications so you can make good decisions about the value and mode of each communication.

First jot some notes on your current skills in the following areas. Base your notes on feedback you have had at work, what you have learned in this book, or any other source of feedback (like personality assessments or coaching).

Topic	Notes
Degree of communication awareness	
The three spheres of communication	
Preparing yourself and others	
Your communication style	
Communication filters	
Internal dialogue (self-talk)	
Power and credibility	
Empathy with the audience; making connections	
Your company communication culture	
Building rapport	
Resolving conflict	
Your conflict communication style	
Your messages: simplicity, clarity, logic	
Written communication	
Speaking	
Presentation skills	
Non-verbal communication	
Voice and emotional expressiveness	
Checking for understanding	

Rank the areas you want to work on in order of priority. For each priority above, write a vision statement that creates as clear a picture as possible of your desired state. Don't skip over any part of this step. It is a vital part of motivating yourself and achieving your goals. Imagine yourself in your desired state.

Milestone	What I want to achieve
In one month	
In six months	
In one year	
In 5 years	
In 10 years	
In 15 years	
In 20 years	

Ask yourself these questions:

1 What will I be able to do that I cannot do now?
2 How will I feel?
3 What skills will I have that I don't have now?
4 How will I know I have reached that state?
5 What feedback will I receive that tells me I've succeeded?
6 How will my management life look if I don't learn these new skills?
7 How will failure impact my career?

Now put together an action plan, using a form like the one below.

Name:	Date:
My short- and long-term communication vision	My model(s) (Who can I model my communication after?)
The communication challenge, desire, obstacle	Solutions and steps
Target dates	How I will reward myself for reaching the targets
How I will measure progress	How I will know I have succeeded

Repeat this for the three most important areas where you would like to improve your management communication skills. This is not an exercise to complete, print and file in a drawer. Review it regularly, modify it, and share it with your colleagues and superiors so they can help you achieve your vision. Even a small improvement can take you far.

 Briefing Lessons

To improve the effectiveness of every interpersonal communication, managers should follow a three-step process.

Step 1: Prepare yourself and the receiver(s)

Strategic questions:

- **What is the purpose of my communication?**
- **What do I want my audience to do (determine an observable, measurable action, if possible)?**
- **What channel will be most effective for this audience in this context?**
- **What is my key message?**

Clear away obstacles to communication:

- **Control your inner critic, build positive intent.**
- **Examine assumptions.**
- **Reflect on your power position, credibility and influence.**
- **Be aware of significant communication filters.**

Step 2: Send your message

- **Craft a simple, well-structured key message.**
- **Choose a rhetorical strategy.**
  - **Test your reasoning.**
  - **Test your evidence.**
- **Make your message SMART:**
  - **Specific**
  - **Measurable**
  - **Actionable**
  - **Realistic**
  - **Time stamped.**

- If you're giving a presentation, make it audience centred (see the checklist).
- Consider using a story to engage the audience.
- Be assertive, not aggressive.

Step 3: Check for understanding

- Listen actively.
- Build rapport.
- Get and give feedback consciously.
- Resolve conflicts quickly.
- Be aware of hidden agendas.

Internal communication

6

- Introduction

- Step 1: Prepare yourself and the company employees (receivers)

- Step 2: Send your message

- Step 3: Check for understanding

- Prepare a strategic communication plan for reaching employees

Introduction

It is not enough for you to be an effective communicator with the individuals you manage. You need to be effective in the larger groups in which you operate: teams, business units, regions, divisions, whole companies. No matter what the company communication guidelines, you have a vital role in developing broad business understanding, as well as maintaining a positive and inclusive work environment and a motivated workforce. Here, communication can be a vital function.

To get employee communication right, you should also follow the three-step communication model: (1) prepare yourself and the receiver, (2) send your message and (3) check for understanding. The difference between applying the model in employee communication and applying it in one-on-one or small group (interpersonal) communication is that your receivers are groups of employees. Nevertheless, thinking of your communication as a three-step process will again help you to become more effective.

Most successful companies make employee communications a fundamental and significant element of their communications activities. In such companies, managers work hard on their employee communications. They work closely with their companies' internal communications people. They create an environment conducive to the open exchange of information and conversation, in line with the spirit of their company's core values (assuming it has articulated them), code of business conduct and business challenges.

Effective employee communication is not just the ken of the CEO and a small cadre of senior managers. It is the responsibility of all managers. Everyone in the company is responsible for sharing information appropriately and for actively participating in the communication process. All employees must feel responsible for keeping themselves informed and for communicating openly in target-setting sessions and performance reviews.

Below we will go through the three-step communication model as it applies to company internal communication.

Step 1: Prepare yourself and the company employees (receivers)

Many managers' communication with groups of employees is less effective than it needs to be because they don't prepare themselves well, or take a long view that encompasses all three steps in the three-step model. Some prepare well and send clear messages, but don't check for understanding. Others prepare themselves but don't send clear messages, and yet others prepare little, winging their communication even to large groups of employees. In hard times, it is all too easy to get caught up with investors, analysts, the media, suppliers and retailers, and thereby overlook employees at precisely the time you should be communicating more with them. Another reason employee communication may be weak is that many managers hold beliefs that block good communication. Here are a few tips for avoiding these communication traps.

Tips

- **Effective internal communications is a purposeful, strategic campaign.** From now on, think of all your communication as one long campaign, much like a political campaign. You need to be clear about your key messages, and you must communicate them consistently in words, non-verbal signals and actions.

- **Never assume that communication just happens.** Don't get caught thinking, 'I told everyone, or at least the key people… that's enough!' Be aware of what you told to whom – even when you intended for everyone to know the information.

- **Check that employees got your intended message.** With diversity in the workforce increasing, it's easy to believe you've conveyed information to someone, but you aren't aware that they interpreted you differently from how you intended. Unfortunately, you won't be aware of this problem until a major issue arises out of the confusion.

- **In times of stress, listen, listen, listen.** Particularly when personnel are tired or under stress, it's easy to do what's urgent rather than what's important. So people misunderstand others' points or intentions. This problem usually gets discovered too late. Keep your ears to the employee grapevine, and make sure people are hearing your messages about what is important.

- **As your business grows, you need to communicate more frequently.** When organisations are just getting started, their managers may pride themselves on not being burdened with what seems like bureaucratic overhead – extensive written policies and procedures. Writing things down can be seen as a sign of bureaucracy. But as any organisation grows, it needs more communication and feedback to remain healthy, but this communication isn't valued. As a result, increasing confusion ensues.

- **Communicate even when there is no problem to be solved.** Communications problems can arise when inexperienced managers interpret their job to be solving problems and if there aren't any problems or crises, then there's nothing that needs to be communicated.

- **Don't confuse passing on information with communication.** As organisations grow, their management tends to focus on matters of efficiency. They often generate systems that produce substantial amounts of data – raw information that doesn't seem to be really important or relevant.

- **Work toward an open communication climate.** Create a company communication climate in which employees can say what they think without fear of retribution or dismissal. Promote open dialogue. Encourage feedback.

Listen actively. Put the 'undiscussables' on the table. Work toward transparency. Aim for trust and honesty, within the framework of company, local and national culture.

- **Tell them in advance.** If your message affects people where they live and breathe, get it out sooner rather than later. Whether you're dealing with salespeople, janitors or top management, anytime you need to make a decision that affects people's lives, tell them well in advance of the event taking place. Examples are change programmes, benefits and HR policies.

- **Give enough information.** Some managers think that the less said the better. Problem: our minds mind are always asking the never-ending question 'Why?' So, always provide sufficient information for the employee to be able to answer the question 'Why?' Make sure employees know what you know. Don't assume that because you are aware of some piece of information, everyone else is, too. Consider using open book management: show everybody where the company's money went, that expenses have risen and that profits are down. While there may be things you cannot share, for legal or ethical reasons, provide employees with enough information that would allow them to draw similar conclusions if they were in your position. Usually employees aren't aware unless management makes a deliberate attempt to carefully convey information.

- **Your messages must be congruent.** Act congruently with the message that you project. Be aware of your non-verbal communication at all times: not just facial expressions and gestures, but also symbolic actions and behaviours that send a public signal. Employees will notice in seconds if your actions belie your message.

The boss who tries to convince his people how important dedication to the job is and then is seen leaving the office at noon every Friday in the summer carrying a set of golf clubs is not very persuasive or effective.

Prepare by building trust and engagement

There are three issues to be considered as part of preparing employees for communication:

- trust
- a common agenda
- dialogue.

Figure 6.1 shows the three key issues with their common elements.

Figure 6.1 The three issues

Trust
openess
frankness
honesty

Dialogue
continuous
communication

Common agenda
shared goals
and vision

Prepare by building trust and engagement

Good managers engage people, not only through communication *per se*, but also through the relationships they have with all stakeholders, such that they gain commitment rather than trying to force compliance. Good relationships are predicated on trust, shared understanding of a common agenda and a dialogue that offers a two-way exchange of valuable and relevant information. None of this is possible in the absence of open, frank communication.

When employees trust you, they trust your communication. They believe in your reliability, truth, ability or strength. They acccept what you say without evidence or investigation. When you say that the company is doing well, you want your employees to believe you. They rely on your word on matters over which they have no control. The believe you will be frank, open and honest with them while treating each other with respect.

Sadly, this is not always the case. Enron's Kenneth Lay was telling his employees the company was in great shape, even as it was sliding into a morass. The top management of Bear Sterns told its employees that all was well, even when they knew that a run on the bank was sending the once-revered investment bank over the brink of bankruptcy.

Your employee communication should be based on ongoing dialogue, not just a once-a-year annual performance review (an oxymoron, since performance review should be an ongoing, regular activity, with no surprises). Your dialogue should stem from a common agenda – shared goals and a vision. When you and your employees share a goal, you are more likely than not to be able to resolve a conflict calmly and wisely. Here are some tips for your ongoing dialogue.

Tips

- **Be direct and clear while also being diplomatic.**
- **Show tact and respect.**
- **Share your visions and goals.**
- **Be sincere, honest and up-front.**

Consider the following examples:

Raw:	'That's never going to work.'
Polished:	'Can you tell me more about what you're proposing? I'm having a difficult time seeing how it will improve the situation.'
Raw:	'You're keeping me out of the loop.'
Polished:	'I'm sensing you feel I shouldn't be involved in this project.'
Raw:	'You'll never make the client happy with that approach.'
Polished:	'I know we all want to make certain the client is satisfied, and I have some concerns about the approach you're proposing.'
Raw:	'I think you're mistaken and my suggestions will work better.'
Polished:	'I understand your viewpoint, and I'd like to share mine with you now.'
Raw:	'I really have to tell you this before we start.'
Polished:	'Before we start, I'd like to share some information about myself with you.'

Build your communication credibility and a common agenda with all employees

Credibility is vital to you because much of your job is to persuade people to do things. Low credibility can cause frustrating inaction, widespread cynicism, and low or unsustainable performance. Whether corporate initiatives succeed may depend heavily on people understanding the reason for change, financial criteria, process and operational changes. Often change initiatives fail to have the desired impact because of a manager's lack of credibility. Even if you are communicating consistently and regularly, you may lack credibility. Lack of credibility may make any communication ineffective, leading to low engagement and lack of results.

Your aim should be consistent, credible communication. Your actions should match your words. Match what you say with what you do. Your credibility with a given audience (credibility is always in the eye of the beholder) frequently affects the success or failure of arguments. There are five main sources of credibility:

1 rank or status (your position in the company hierarchy)

2 goodwill

3 expertise

4 image or identification

5 morality or fairness.

You have a certain amount of credibility with your employees before you communicate (that amount may be zero or negative). Your communication itself can affect certain types of credibility. For example, if you are a new manager, or you are addressing a group that doesn't know you well, you can establish credibility through expertise by citing credentials and demonstrating knowledge. You can establish or boost credibility through fairness by presenting a balanced argument. Conversely, you can damage your credibility in a communication that demonstrates lack of expertise or fairness, or that projects a bureaucratic and stuffy image.

Credibility increases rapport. It can also help build a common agenda. A speaker who has credibility with an auditorium full of employees can build rapport more easily than if credibility is lacking. Remember, too, that the people above you in the organisation hierarchy expect a certain behaviour from you. When they receive it they tend to give you more credibility. Beware of the difference between 'kissing up' and earning respect with your employees.

Ask yourself:

- Do you have credibility with people in power in your company?
- Do you have credibility with the people who work for you?
- What is the source of your credibility?
- Does your communication increase or decrease your credibility with them?
- What can you do to increase or enhance your credibility with key stakeholders?

Another way to build credibility is active listening. Listen and respond openly and honestly to employees. Treat employees' questions or complaints constructively, including problem evaluation, concerns, progress and project results, as appropriate. Encourage your employees to communicate issues such as:

- opinions of the company and their jobs
- interpretations of problems and opportunities at the company
- suggestions about the company's business, its specific programmes, policies and procedures
- aspirations for their career or job development.

Encourage dialogue

Publish an employee communication policy

Your company needs an employee communication policy. It should promote open dialogue. If you don't have one, write one. Here's a fictitious corporate example:

> Company Q believes in the freedom of information, consistent with the need to protect our and third parties' confidential information, and encourages open communication across all levels. The company commits to providing timely and accurate information on key matters. Company Q expects all employees to take responsibility for remaining informed about the company's business.
>
> The company encourages open communication, particularly between employees and their immediate managers. Company Q intends to give consistent information, to use the most efficient distribution channels available, and to maintain effective employee communication vehicles to support and supplement manager–employee communications. Managers are responsible for achieving the objectives of this policy with their departments. They are responsible for building and supporting an environment that encourages the open exchange of information, and for making certain the information they communicate is coherent, consistent and continuous.

Publish communication guidelines for all managers

Communication guidelines for managers should rest on the following principles:

- effective communication should be everyone's concern
- two-way, open communication
- powerful, open dialogue.

Employees contribute interest, commitment and engagement. Employees should also actively seek and share valuable information, which will positively affect their abilty to perform at work, and ensure that they have the information they need to get their work done. The company communications function is responsible for supporting managers and top management, getting communications aligned with marketing, human resources or other units, depending on the area. The communications department is – or should be – responsible for the infrastructure, ensuring that communications channels are effective.

Nevertheless, *you* are the driver of effective communication. Here are some effective tips.

Tips

- Build an employee communications plan that takes advantage of existing channels and provides a communication link to employees.
- Communicate the company vision, mission, goals, objectives, strategy, business information, department goals and central initiatives.
- Communicate job responsibilities and information about how each employee's job contributes to company success.
- Ensure that the company's core values, code of business conduct and people are understood.
- Provide relevancy, motivation and guidance. You are responsible for communicating company goals and strategies, job responsibilities and how they contribute to company success.
- Complete yearly employee appraisals in a spirit of active listening, checking assumptions, resolving conflicts and open dialogue.
- Explain company policies and procedures and discuss employee career development and training needs.
- Encourage employees to give constructive feedback without fear of reprisals.
- Hold regularly scheduled meetings with employees.

Step 2: Send your message

An international drug company, with headquarters in Germany, decided to merge two of its sales teams: the one from its generic drug unit in China, based in Beijing, and the other its heart and blood pressure medication sales team, based in Shanghai, under one global sales function. The two sales teams understand well the rationale for the decision: cost savings, efficiency, a redeployment of sales people in the weakening Asian market and a projected 15 per cent yearly growth in the sector. The decision was announced to the two Chinese teams in an email, and then cascaded by managers to their sales sub-units. The various personnel policies, sales approaches and strategies differed widely.

Six months after the official merger, the new team lacked identity, many sales people did not understand the reasons for the merger, some were unhappy about the changes in their compensation packages, and others struggled to apply the new sales approaches. And since the entire merger had been 'rushed' by the management at HQ, the new sales targets for the newly merged team appeared, at least to members of those teams, to be impossible to reach.

The net effect: low morale, high anxiety, and performance below top management expectations. More effective communication could have helped this fictitous company, as it could in countless real-life scenarios.

Answer the six common employee questions

The effect of poor internal communications can be seen at its most destructive in global organisations that suffer from employee annexation – where the head office in one country is buoyant (since they are closest to the action, know what is going on, and are heavily engaged) but its annexes (who are furthest away from the action and know little about what is happening) are disengaged. In the worst case, employee annexation can be very destructive when the head office attributes the annex's low engagement to its poor performance... when its poor performance is really due to its poor communications.

Effective employee communications convey a clear description of 'what's going on', 'why', 'how we did and what it means' and 'where we're headed' – see Figure 6.2.

Figure 6.2 The essential employee questions

How can I help?
Do employees know what they
can and can't do to help?

What's my job?
Do all employees know exactly
what is expected of them?

**What's our
vision, mission
and values?**
Do employees
understand?

**How am
I doing?**
What sort of
feedback do
employees get?

How are WE doing?
Do employees understand team and
departments of rent goals and get results?

Does anyone care?
Do individuals and teams get
adequate recognition and thanks?

Employees tend to ask these same questions and seek the same information. If you address them often and answer them clearly, you will motivate your employees. Giving employees a satisfying answer to each question requires that you seek dialogue and practise effective feedback. Many managers start their communications by answering the question: where are we heading? This seems natural, as it is one of the key questions on their minds. Their quarterly and yearly targets are determined by the company's direction. Further, many of the top management team have access to strategic information, take part in discussions of strategy, and often talk about it with colleagues and their bosses. But managers often leave out the other burning employee questions.

The idea is not to answer such questions in every message, every email, every meeting agenda, but rather, that in your overall communications planning, you must ensure that your employees can answer these questions to their own satisfaction. The best way to find out how well you are putting these steps into practice is to run a communications audit: a simple questionnaire to find out to what extent your stakeholders are satisfied with your answers and your communication approaches.

A communications audit

1. **What is my job?** The first question is about providing clear expectations for the employee's specific job. In other words: what do you expect from him or her? An employee cannot help management meet its end of the company 'deal' if he doesn't understand specifically what the management wants. Though it may appear to be motivating for bright, ambitious employees to be told, 'Do whatever you know makes sense and that will move us forward', that employee is likely to lose motivation if whatever he chooses to do does not meet the manager's expectations, no matter how well it may have been executed. The employee who is told to 'come up with a marketing strategy as soon as possible' will do whatever she thinks makes sense, according to her understanding of the company context, strategy, performance, etc. But she is also likely to be shattered to hear from her manager, 'This is way too complicated. This isn't what I wanted.'

2. **How am I doing?** Answering this question ensures that you provide effective feedback regularly so that people know how they are doing in their jobs. If there is an issue, question, concern or criticism, the employee should be aware of it before one of the regularly scheduled performance appraisals. And if employees are doing well, they should be hearing it regularly, and not just once in a performance review. How many times have you heard stories of employees getting a bonus cheque from their manager without a word of thanks, or appreciation? Give specific feedback. It is not enough for the manager to say, 'Great job! Excellent work.' Say, instead, 'You did a great job redesigning the website to make it more user friendly and to make online payments simpler and easier. And all that, within budget. You're a valuable asset to this company.'

3. **Does it matter?** People need to know how their job, function or role fits into the bigger picture: there is little point in committing yourself to high performance if what you are doing adds no value, or isn't valued by the

company. I was once involved in a survey that asked the more than 400 employees in an educational services provider how their work contributed to the success of the organisation. Only 17 per cent could describe why customers attended programmes at this institution and how their own work contributed to company success. This startlingly low percentage reflected a failure of communication between the middle management and the employees in their teams. A majority of non-management employees stated that they 'do what their manager tells them'.

4. **How are 'we' doing?** Once people understand the quality of their own performance, they want to learn about the team's, group's, unit's or division's performance and expectations. At one time or another, every employee asks: how is the company doing? What are our results and what do they mean for us, and for me?

5. **Where are we heading?** To perform well, all employees need to understand the company direction and how their work fits into the overall pictures and activity.

6. **How can I help?** When all of the above five questions have been covered – and they should be covered regularly – empowerment comes naturally. When people understand the competitive environment, the company positioning, their role in company success, the company strategy, the market, etc., they can think proactively about how they can contribute their distinctive talents.

Disseminating company information employees need

Although information is not communication *per se*, it is a key component of communication. Employees at all levels need varying degrees of information to help them meet performance objectives, and contribute to and achieve company and department goals. They must also take responsibility for getting information they think is important.

Information should be considered open to all employees unless stated differently (when this is the case, strong reasons should be available). Employees working on confidential projects should be clear about the sensitivities involved and the levels of detail at which they can discuss the project, and with whom. If it could jeopardise the company's competitive position, business goals, or business relationships, information should be withheld unless specific employees need to know the information to do their jobs. Every company should have clear policies regarding confidentiality, and all managers should take it seriously. To ensure that information is available to those who need it when they need it:

● Take responsibility for ensuring that all employees have the information they need.

● Cascade information in a systematic, structured way. Encourage everyone to be responsible for sharing information as appropriate and for actively participating in the communication process.

- Carry responsibility for disseminating information about important and relevant changes in the organisation, business developments and many other things – crises, developments related to the media – that help keep employees feel more motivated and engaged.
- Disseminate information about relevant organisational changes, the company's strategic directions and business developments.

Disseminate information through vehicles you know will reach your employees:

- newsletters
- bulletin boards
- blogs (video and text)
- podcasts
- videos
- brochures
- presentations

- town halls
- mass email
- intranet postings
- wikis /ftp files
- social networking sites
- RSS feeds.

Say a lot, do a lot

Think about your communication 'positioning' by using the matrix shown in Figure 6.3. You want to get to the upper right quadrant, where communication is frequent, and also tied directly to company strategy and goals. The old suggestion: communicate, communicate, communicate is useless, or even harmful, if the communication isn't moving the company toward its desired results.

Figure 6.3 A positioning matrix

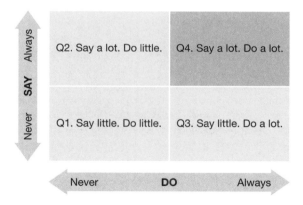

The manager in quadrant 1 says little and does little. Employees lose interest quickly. A quadrant 2 manager talks a lot but delivers little, and quickly loses credibility among employees. The result: trust sinks, and employees resist doing what the manager wants done. The manager in quadrant 3 works hard and is action-oriented but tends not to keep people informed and well aware of what is happening. This approach leads to speculation and mistrust: employees assume that 'things are happening behind closed doors', and that these things are probably not in their best interests.

Combining the skills of quadrants 2 and 3 is where you want to be: quadrant 4, the upper right. This communication combination leads to consistent, credible communication, based on understanding and respect among employees. A key factor in getting to quadrant 4 is credibility.

There are some questions to ask yourself about your credibility, whenever you are preparing an employee communication, or a communication plan:

1 How much credibility do you have with the audience?
2 What are the sources of that credibility?
   ● Position within the company?
   ● Technical expertise?
   ● Your 'track record'?
   ● Relationships with key people?
   ● Personal characteristics?
   ● Values similar to those of the audience?
3 How can you increase or reinforce your credibility with the audience? Or with the people among your important stakeholders?

Create opportunities to deliver key messages

Your communication is an ongoing dialogue or conversation: there is no end to the messaging, whether in the board room or the canteen, in the conference room or in the parking area. Your messaging must be aligned with company goals and strategies, and you must stay on message. This is not to advocate manipulation or turning your communication into the equivalent of a cynical political campaign; nevertheless, the effective communicator is keenly aware that he or she is always communicating. Work to ensure that you always send the key messages you need to send.

To disperse your messages, seek and create frequent opportunities for interaction and communication with your employees and, wherever possible, use these opportunities for business-related information. Coffee machine chats are nice – they can build commitment and give you a 'human touch' – but bringing *business-related information* into your coffee group will help the company realise its strategic goals. By creating opportunities to share business-related communication, you can involve employees in co-creating certain activities and plans, answer questions, tame the grapevine, clarify, put doubts to rest and gain engagement. The purpose of your communication should be to:

- Cascade information in a systematic, structured way.
- Build an employee communications culture and processes that take advantage of existing channels and provide a communication link to employees.
- Encourage employees to give constructive feedback without fear of reprisals.
- Communicate the company vision, mission, objectives, strategy, business information, department goals, central initiatives.
- Ensure that the company's core values, code of business conduct and people (idea) are understood.
- Built trust in regularly scheduled meetings with your employees.
- Share and leverage best practices. Work in partnership with your colleagues. Build cooperative relationships in your department and between functions.
- Share support systems, networks and resources and work to reduce duplicated or redundant efforts.
- Share ideas, best practices and learning in both an informal and a more formal manner.
- Work toward collaborative relationships across the company.

Create strategic messages for employees

Linking communication and strategy is vital to your management – and company – success. Communicating effectively with all employees in your area of responsibility requires preparation, planning and a long-term perspective. You need to identify your long-term, overall aims and interests and the best means of communicating to achieve them. You need a communications plan that best serves your long-term company objectives. In your plan, every communication needs a clear purpose that serves the company strategy. It is hard, detailed work, and effectiveness is hard to measure, but without judicious planning, your communications will be spotty and haphazard, reactive, and unlikely to fuel your results.

At Tetra Pak, one of the world's largest and most successful food processing and packaging companies (20,000 employees in more than 150 markets), employees and managers use a simple acronym ('PACK') to form the basis of a powerful 'preparation model' for all communications:

P = Purpose
A = Audience
C = Channels
K = Key messages.

Applying this simple tool in your daily management activity will help you be more effective, especially if you know how each message formulated with PACK fits into your larger communication strategy and serves the company strategy.

For every message to employees: a purpose

The following questions need to be asked:

- Why are you doing this?
- What do you want to achieve?
- What do you want the audience to do?
- How does the purpose support the overall business objectives?
- What is it supposed to change? Is it all a problem related to information or communication?
- In what way can information/communication activities lead to increased understanding, knowledge or a positive attitude and how will that contribute to overall business objectives?
- Is the issue old, complex and/or emotional. Are you trying to increase people's knowledge or trying to change their behaviour? What, exactly, are you trying to change? And what do you want the audience to think, feel, believe or do?

For every message to employees: a clearly defined employee audience

An audience comprises people with similar interests, need or demands under similar circumstances. Consider what you want them to think, feel, believe and, most importantly, do. When you define your audience, look at them from the viewpoint of their interest in what you are doing. Put yourself in their shoes. Think not about what you want to say, but what you would like them to remember.

- Who is your audience?
- What is particular about that audience (position, knowledge, culture, etc.)?
- What do you want them to think, believe, feel or do?
- Is your communication relevant to them? How? Why?
- Does it have consequences for them? What are they?
- Will they care? Should they care?
- What is their predicament – their state of mind today?
- What's in it for them? What's their 'so what'?

Determine your groups by level of knowledge about the issue you're communicating or by position. Often these two groups overlap: senior people inside the company have the same level of knowledge, for example. Members of the IT business unit share certain knowledge about the company's IT systems. Other factors to consider are education, origin, culture, gender and age.

You can also define your audience(s) by doing a simple stakeholder analysis, much the way marketing people do. This exercise will help you define the various target groups for your messages, and then determine what you need to say to each group, and how.

A simple stakeholder map gives you a way of thinking about your various audiences, whether they are inside the company (employees, top management, the legal department, etc.) or outside the company. Draw the groups inside circles, for example. This will enable you to define all your communication stakeholders, both employees, your first concern, and people outside the company, like your suppliers and your customers. To be effective, you need to prioritise them. Which ones will you communicate with regularly and which ones will you communicate with on an ad hoc basis? Make sure your communication strategy is integrated across all your stakeholders, with your messages adapted for each audience.

The three groups of company stakeholders

Think of your stakeholders as roughly divided into three groups (see Figure 6.4):

1 Those that are internal and therefore part of your employee communications.
2 Those that are external and relate to marketing communications.
3 Those that are external and relate to professional, governmental, investor, community or environmental activities.

Figure 6.4 The three main stakeholder groups

Here some typical examples of stakeholders in each group:

Employee communications	Marketing communications	Corporate affairs
Potential employees	Suppliers	Local authorities
Employees	Customers	Global authorities
Contractors	Retailers	Opinion makers
Union and workers' council	Consumers	Local media
Temporary employees	Competitors	Global media
Regions		Trade media
Divisions and units		Professional organisations
Board		Local 'neighbours'
Owners (if private)		Financiers and investors

For every message to employees: a clearly defined internal channel

Communication channels refer to all opportunities of sending messages or establishing communication. A channel could be internal as well as external (mass media, for example), but it can also refer to conversations, personal meetings, town halls, webinars, podcasts, video blogs, text blogs, email, social networking sites (Facebook, Twitter), memos, electronic notice boards, conferences, seminars, press conferences, presentations, presentations, press releases, trade shows, etc.

Choose the channels that will reach your defined audiences most effectively. Remember: conversations and meetings are channels. No matter how well you execute the formal channels of communication such as newsletters, email, text messaging, voice mail, videos, blogs, webinars, charts, while they can inform, clarify and influence the audience, you get, at best, a modicum of involvement. If you want to involve and engage people deeply, really spark their interest and send them messages that 'stick' and motivate them to action, you need to communicate face-to-face. Face-to-face, eye-to-eye and, in some cases, social media is your best chance for commitment and action.

 Tip

Back up your face-to-face communication with support materials so people can read, reflect and seek out answers to questions they may have and also to ensure that the messages they are receiving are consistent.

Choose channels that will boost the impact of your messages and make sure you utilise the full potential of the chosen channel. All channels have pros and cons. Some complement each other. For example, you may use a company town hall to kick-off an initiative, followed by email reminders with links to internet information pages and regular update postings; internet interviews with key players; short video clips giving the senior view; posters in offices around the world; and desk drops (items like calendars and laminated cards that remind people of key messages).

In choosing channels, your aim is to reach your desired target group. The channels you choose should be perceived as credible. If they are perceived as untruthful or unimportant, your message will probably share the same fate. For millenials, social media is a trusted channel. If you manage a London Hedge Fund, and the data from an employee engagement survey reveals that your traders regularly delete every email that doesn't come from clients or direct bosses, make sure that important informational emails come from the direct boss, and not from a distant, 'irrelevant' (to the traders) manager. If members of your sales team are on the road 80 per cent of the time, with patchy access to broadband connections, and they receive, on average, 150 emails a day, do not send one email with vital company information and assume that the sales force will read it.

Some channels have 'owners': editors or producers who work inside the company. There are many such owners in large company communications, branding and marketing departments. Form alliances with them so that they understand your concerns and priorities and so that you understand their requirements, such as release dates, scope, policy, etc. Armed with that information, it is possible for you to align your key messages with the channels you have chosen. You can also consider how the channels can support each other by referring to each other (this is easy with internet and intranet site linking) and how a message can gain 'weight' and credibility by choosing the right spokesperson.

Questions to ask include:

- Which channels work best for the audience and the purpose?
- How could you use different channels to support and complement one another?
- Which is your leading channel and which are the supporting ones?

Create a portfolio of key messages for employees

You need a portfolio of key messages you can send and repeat. They must support company strategy and serve business objectives. They should help employees reach company targets. Each one should be simple and clear (refer to the section of the book on creating key messages). Boil down your key messages to no more than three sentences each – one is better. They should fit on one sheet of A4 paper. Or one each on a 3 × 5 card. These are the messages you repeat regularly, in a purposeful way. Every presentation, newsletter or email should carry them, or at least echo them. Each key message can be phrased and expressed in numerous ways but all your key messages should have the same core and intent.

You may change the messages after some time, but make the change consciously – know your purpose. Imagine you want to tell four different audiences that you have implemented a new payment system. Each message should be cast in terms of the benefits for the particular audience. Here's how the messages may look.

Audience	Key message
CEO or similar	*Good news*: project delivered on time, within budget, with added efficiency, and a projected savings of $3.5 million over three years.
Shareholders	*Good news*: State-of-the art payment system is a good investment. In the years 2010 to 2012, it will produce significant yields.
Customers	*Good news*: You can now pay us online. Benefits to you are ease of navigation, higher online payment security, faster fulfilment of your order and a more reliable order-tracking system.
Employees	*Good news*: our new state-of-the-art payment system makes us the first to offer such a system, and we expect it to boost revenues, attract customers, and make it easier for you to focus on your main job – customer service.

 Tips

When you prepare the key messages for every communication, always ask:

- **What do you want your audience to remember (think, feel, believe, do)?**
- **Are your messages understandable and linked to the business?**
- **Have you supported your messages with examples and facts?**

Reaching widely dispersed employees

The US division of the accounting firm Deloitte began exploring social media when communicators realised that the average age of its workforce was 27, which meant that employees were already using social media tools outside the office. So Deloitte created an internal Facebook-like social networking site called D-Street, which was quickly adopted by employees eager to connect with each other.

The situation was quite different at a major insurance company with a growing segment of employees working remotely. At this company, most remote employees were baby boomers (born between 1946 and 1962). So social media didn't necessarily come naturally to them. The company focused its efforts on providing collaboration tools (such as wikis or work-group sites) that appealed to employees' need to get work done, not get to know one another.

More and more employees are working in far-away locations, at home, from airports, hotels, buses, trains, planes and even from Starbucks. They work alone, in small groups and teams, in centres of excellence. In 2009, it was estimated that up to 10 per cent of employees used telecommuting, triple the number that did so in 2000. And 82 per cent of senior executives expect that the number of employees who work remotely will increase over the coming years. These employees have one thing in common: they need to stay in touch with their widely dispersed colleagues, and they need to get regular communication from their managers and from divisional, regional and global headquarters. The challenge is to keep remote workers feeling connected – to managers, peers and the organisation – despite physical distance and lack of face-to-face contact.

Here are some main points to consider:

1 **Analyse your off-site employee audiences.** The more you understand about who your remote workers are (demographics, job responsibilities, locations), what they think, feel and need, the better you can design a social media solution that works for you and for them. Remote employees most often cite these challenges: workplace isolation, lack of face-to-face communication and low visibility to their boss or co-workers. By identifying your employees' most pressing challenges, you can choose solutions that best address them.

2 **Choose the right tool for the job.** The social media universe offers a dizzying array of choices. It can be difficult to know which tool to use for which purpose. At IMB, the global IT and consulting company, more than 42 per cent of its 400,000 employees work remotely at least part of the time, and 15 per cent work *solely* from home. IBM has discovered that each social media tool serves a distinct purpose. For example, the company uses:

   ● A wiki to allow employees to collaborate.
   ● Blogs to give employees an opportunity to share their knowledge and perspectives and allow others to comment and participate. (At IBM, 17,000 employees manage internal blogs!)
   ● Microblogging (as in Twitter) to duplicate the 'water cooler' experience of employees engaged in casual conversation about what they're working on.
   ● Social networking (*à la* Facebook) to build relationships.

3 **Test, launch, adjust and reinforce.** Social media is a moving target. It is always evolving. Many managers prefer their communication to be more controlled (some businesses, like financial services organisations, need to worry about confidentiality and control). Employees contribute and shape social media, making it an unpredictable experience. That's especially true when dealing with remote workers who are themselves in motion. To communicate with remote workers, you can't just build a social networking platform and hope employees will come. Even the most intriguing social media tool needs to be launched with some fanfare to get employees' attention. Then you need to keep communicating about the tool until your workers try it out, see the value and grow accustomed to using it.

As employees' needs and experiences change, change your company's use of social media. Take a lesson from Best Buy, the electronics retailer (the first UK stores opened in 2010). When Best Buy first introduced an intranet site called Blue Shirt Nation for store employees, its goal was to give its remote employees – who work at more than 1,100 stores worldwide – a platform for sharing best practice to better serve customers. But employees quickly started using the site to connect with co-workers throughout the organisation. So the company's communications people changed Blue Shirt Nation to fit employees' needs. Today, the site includes:

- An online discussion forum where employees share information about any topic.
- An area to post innovative ideas and gain feedback from peers, and gain approval for those ideas.
- A prediction market tool that allows employees to vote on concepts and predict business results.
- Wikis on a variety of customer issues that allow employees to add and edit based on their experiences.

Social media can replicate the informal interactions that naturally occur when employees work at the same location. Twitter, wikis and social networking sites can:

- Help you explain the company's goals, values and strategy.
- Give you easy ways to stay connected with your team members, even if they are in Mumbai, Warsaw and Miami.
- Increase your visibility and accessibility.
- Allow your employees to share ideas and help each other solve problems.
- Create opportunities for feedback and two-way communication.

The following chart lists the most common social networking channels, and describes in brief how they work, what their advantages and disadvantages are, their best use and some tips for their application.

Instant messaging (IM)

How it works	Sends and receives written messages inside a single pop-up screen shared by two or more users. Users with desktop, laptop or smartphone cameras can use video chat.
Advantages	Remote workers feel like they're in the office. Faster and more intimate than email. You can see who's online. Tracks and transcribes exchanges. Often used for non-urgent matters with the expectation of an immediate response.
Disadvantages	Distracting, perhaps too easy for colleagues to see who's online. Not good for detailed conversations. Often not secure.
Best used for	Immediate feedback. Quick question-and-answer exchanges. Seeing if someone is available for a phone call. Sending links during a conference call. Reminders or alerts. ('I just emailed you the file.')
Tips	Find a good programme, like Trillian or Adium, that supports multiple IM clients. If you're getting too many IMs, change your setting to 'invisible', create separate IM addresses for personal and professional use, and tell colleagues that you prefer to use IM for urgent issues only.

Personal digital assistant (PDA) Smartphone

How it works	Bundles phone, email, calendar, applications and other features into one hand-held device, like BlackBerry and iPhone.
Advantages	You're always connected. Stay on top of things while not at your computer and office. You don't need to sync the device like the old days.
Disadvantages	You're always connected. Small size makes typing slow, and screens can be hard to read. Brevity of emails you send can be misinterpreted as curt or overly direct.
Best used for	Managers who need constant access to email and calendar, especially when travelling.
Tips	Set guidelines for when you'll use it and when you won't.

Teleconference

How it works	Allows many users to dial into a phone call. Can be hosted internally or through a third-party service provider.
Advantages	Connects many people simultaneously. Real time. Inexpensive. More personal than email. Saves travel costs.
Disadvantages	Not always clear who's talking. Time lags may result in people talking at the same time. Callers often multi-task, so their attention is divided. If most of the group is in one location, people calling in may feel left out of the conversation. Hard to show people what you're talking about or give visual presentations.
Best used for	Small groups and teams who know each other. Short meetings.
Tips	Send out an agenda or visual aids before a meeting. Be specific when reviewing visual aids ('At the top of the left column' instead of 'This item over here'). End the call at an agreed time.

Videoconference

How it works	Adds video to a conference call with cameras posted in conference rooms or at individual workstations. Voice activation allows the camera to focus on whoever is speaking.
Advantages	A thrifty alternative to meeting in person. Seeing gestures, expressions, and body language improves communication.
Disadvantages	Needs expensive equipment on both sides. Can be a hassle to set up. Awkward delays and potentially poor sound and/or video quality. With some systems you can see yourself onscreen, which may be distracting for presenters. If your company needs to do simultaneous videoconferences, you need bandwidth of T1 or greater.
Best used for	Scheduled formal meetings when travelling isn't feasible. Team-building across locations. Regular update meetings of teams and departments. Project management meetings. Invaluable for recruiting departments and widely dispersed teams.
Tips	Arrange training for all users of the equipment and request that users on the other end do the same. Set up the call in advance to ensure the meeting will begin on time.

Web conference

How it works	A website or software program like NetMeeting or Webex allows users to meet online in real time. Features include slide presentations, whiteboard annotation, live video, text chat, and real-time audio (using voice over internet protocol (IP)).
Advantages	Improved ability to share documents, so you can show and tell with a remote group. Document mark-up possible.
Disadvantages	Hard to launch and set up if you have large groups and multiple offices. Often relies solely on shared documents for visuals, so you don't get the collaborative feel of videoconferencing.
Best used for	Presentations. Sharing ideas with remote parties. Complicated discussions that require visual diagrams. Troubleshooting with a team. Simple, structured executive development sessions.
Tips	If your charts are boring and your employees are at home or in their cubes, it's easy to lose your audience. Make your visuals dynamic and use polling, messaging, mark-up and brainstorming to keep them engaged.

Wiki or file transfer protocol (FTP) site

How it works	Online archives where you can park large files that colleagues and clients need to access. With a wiki, participants can add and update information to keep the files current.
Advantages	Highly accessible. Wikis allow for linking of documents and make it easy for multiple users to modify files. FTP is better than email for exchanging large files because it keeps them off your email server.
Disadvantages	People often forget to look at a wiki for updates. Not real time. Demands a lot of effort to learn, update and maintain.
Best used for	Gathering feedback, updates and edits from a lot of people on documents. Project planning across many teams.
Tips	To keep a wiki from becoming too long, break sections into separate pages and link them. Designate one person to update the wiki regularly. Set ground rules so people don't override each other's updates.

Collaboration technology

How it works	Project-specific online workspace allows colleagues to exchange and modify information. MeetingPlace is real time and allows one user to share his or her desktop with another. SharePoint doesn't have to be real time, which is good for co-workers in different time zones.
Advantages	Easy to share files and applications. Reduces problems with multiple versions.
Disadvantages	Each member of workgroup needs to download software. Some security risk.
Best used for	Brainstorming. Customer presentations. Storing company and client information in a central location accessible to remote employees.
Tips	Use collaboration technology as a training or repair tool. MeetingPlace allows you to share your desktop, so tech support staff can use it to fix some problems remotely. Since SharePoint is not real time, you may want to use it to work on documents, then launch LiveMeeting to talk about the documents in real time. SharePoint 2007 has a social networking component.

Unified communications

How it works	Software integrates your various communications platforms, including office phone, cell phone, PDA, IM, and email. It builds on voice-over-IP networks and integrates with calendar functions. It can also combine all your messages in one place.
Advantages	Makes you more accessible and potentially more productive by, for example, sending all your office voice mail, cell voice mail, and faxes to your email box.
Disadvantages	People know where you are and what you're doing and expect to be able to reach you at all times. Can cause problems with the performance of other applications on your server.
Best used for	People who travel a lot, and others who carry many devices or receive a lot of communications.
Tips	Before you decide on a unified communications platform, design a complete IT communication strategy. Make sure potential vendors can meet all your needs. Don't expect to switch to voice over IP and unified communications in one step. Consider migrating one technology at a time.

Presence software

How it works	Software links communications devices and calendars to find availability and automatically set up meetings between multiple users.
Advantages	Saves the back and forth communication of trying to set up meetings among busy people.
Disadvantages	You need to update your calendar often, and in granular detail.
Best used for	People with extremely full schedules, teams that have a hard time scheduling meetings.
Tips	Be specific in your calendar entries. If you want colleagues to know you're available for a conference call during a long commute, for example, you need to specify in your calendar entry that you're not in the office but you are available by cell phone.

Telepresence

How it works	A high-definition, high-bandwidth version of videoconferencing. Multiple oversize plasma screens and speakers throughout a conference room and real-time audio give you the closest match to meeting in person, for upwards of £350,000.
Advantages	See expressions and make eye contact. No audio delay. Saves travel costs.
Disadvantages	Cost. Requires dedicated conference rooms, high-bandwidth audio, and voice over IP. Because many systems operate on proprietary networks, they work only for in-company meetings.
Best used for	People who want to cut back on frequent travel.
Tips	Find creative ways to get your money's worth.

Choose the style to get the desired results

There are many diagnostic tools that will help you determine your communication style. One way to think about your communication style is to conceive of various styles in terms of their complexity and the degree to which each style directs people (proposing solutions) or works with them (to develop solutions with them). There are five recognised styles managers can choose to communicate with the people who report to them. Each is appropriate depending on the circumstances (see Figure 6.5).

Figure 6.5 The common communication styles and their complexity

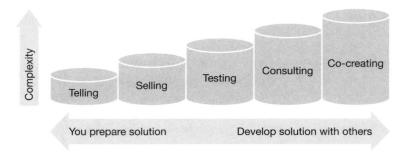

In a crisis, such as a fire in a cocoa warehouse or an outbreak of H1N1, telling people what to do and how to do it is appropriate. However, where it is important to involve and engage support, then a consulting or co-creating approach will be far more effective. Take, for example, a global financial services organisation based in Europe that wants to increase the internal mobility of its most talented employees; that is, the ability of these people to find new challenges and roles that stretch them inside the widely dispersed company. CEO and board members cannot merely tell divisional and regional managers to 'give their best people more mobility', and offer them chances to change positions inside the company. The business heads will resist: after all, why would they want to send their best people away, after training them? Here, the board and top management need to sell the idea in a sort of persuasive campaign – as with any major change programme. They need to consult with the business unit managers and regional heads to find the best way to boost the mobility of the company's best 2,000 employees. Without having a chance to co-create the implementation of the new mobility initiative, the business unit heads and other senior managers will not support the initiative, as it is not in their personal best interest to do so.

A good manager uses each and every one of these styles, depending on the circumstances. The point is that: choosing the right style is a strategic choice.

Tips

The key in making the best choice is this: be aware of your options and conciously select the most appropriate method for the most effective result. Ask yourself these questions:

- What is the purpose of the communication?
- What is the degree of urgency? The more urgent, the more likely you will need to offer a solution.
- What is the communication context?
- What will be the consequences if you don't get the results you need immediately?
- What are the other considerations that may affect your choice of style: hidden agendas, unsurfaced assumptions, undiscussables, conflicts, your degree of credibility, power relationships?

Step 3: Check for understanding

The best way to check for understanding is to ask employees. This starts with the checking skills you use in interpersonal communications: seeking dialogue, building a climate of trust, establishing rapport, and managing every conversation you have at work. The common way to check the understanding of a group of employees is to do research. Run a survey, an employee engagement audit, talk with focus groups of key employees. Later in the book, you will find a discussion of the kinds of research you should consider, with samples of survey and typical questions. The point here is: just as with interpersonal communication, you should get into the habit of finding out, formally and informally, if employees are receiving your messages as you intended, and whether they are getting the desired results.

Prepare a strategic communication plan for reaching employees

Whether you communicate with a team of five or a division of 7,500 people, you need a plan. It can be a rough sketch or a detailed spreadsheet. I have seen one-page communication matrices, but I have also seen 25-page communication concepts. The point is: this is your 'communication play book'. Your plan captures what you will say to whom, when you will say it and how. This is the plan by which you will control your messaging. You should always have it 'top of mind' and 'top of drawer'. This is your map of your short-, medium- and long-term communication activities, though it may contain enough detail to zoom in on the actual single messages. It should span at least the next 12 months.

To construct your personal communication strategy, consider the following steps:

1 Distribute a statement of business objectives to all relevant employees (update this regularly).
2 Assign responsibilities.
3 Create a yearly communication plan.
4 Get management acceptance or sign-off.
5 Select appropriate communication channels.
6 Build a calendar of yearly activities and tie it to your yearly communication plan.
7 Hold kick-off meetings with key people.
8 Tie in your messages and elements of your communication plan with employee engagement data, if you have it.

A success story

Here's an example of a highly effective internal communications concept for a major initiative in the European division of an international software company. We'll call the fictitious company SoftWin. SoftWin wanted to attract, develop and keep the best software engineers and developers, since its pipeline of new products depended entirely on innovations coming from these engineers. They called this initiative Future Titan.

First, the company articulated three key messages to be used by all managers and those responsible for communicating the messages inside and outside the company.

- *Key message 1: The SoftWin vision is to become the most admired software company. This vision drives our aspiration to **attract**, **develop** and **retain** the best talent. The Future Titan initiative is key to realising this aspiration: in today's fierce competition, we can only attract and retain the best talent if we can offer the opportunity for **career growth** and **personal development**.*

- *Key message 2: Through the Future Titan initiative we will drive the implementation of our global **mobility guidelines**, leading to management practices in line with a culture of career development and mobility. We will make job opportunities **transparent** and provide employees with a set of **tools** to support their career development.*

- *Key message 3: Increasing internal mobility is in line with our integrated business strategy and will result in more **engaged**, **knowledgeable** and **loyal employees**: employees who will help our **customers thrive**.*

Note that getting to the three key messages required almost a month of meetings and feedback from more than 30 people in three divisions. Much of this work was done over email and in video and telephone conferences.

Below is the reduced template (matrix) the company used to build its communication plan for the Future Titan initiative. The actual version comprised more than 100 rows. Audiences were grouped by position and then sub-divided by what they needed to know. The messages above were recast for each group, keeping the meaning, but focusing on the particular benefits for each group. Channels were dictated by the company's IT infrastructure and existing communication vehicles. Desk drops and posters were added. Timing was highly granular: whenever possible, the project communication team zeroed in on days and hours, avoiding certain periods, like weekends and Friday afternoons. Comments were notes for the people in charge of implementing the plan. The entire 'campaign' extended for a year from the date of the official announcement (launch) of Project Future Titan. It should be said that this plan was communicated to various levels of management in a different form – in three slides that broke it down into the key areas of interest and concern for that level.

Audience	What they need to know	Message	Messenger	Channels	Timing frequency	Comments

Briefing Lessons

To communicate more effectively with teams, business units, regions, divisions and whole companies, create a strategic communication plan for reaching your employees and apply the three-step model introduced in the previous chapter. Remember:

- Effective employee communication is a purposeful, long-term persuasive campaign.
- Effective messages are consistent, congruent and serve business goals.
- Information is not communication.
- Communicate even when there is no problem: regularly and in advance.
- Build an open communication climate: listening is also communication.

Step 1: Prepare yourself and your receivers

- Articulate three to five key strategic messages.
- Communicate for shared agendas, dialogue and trust.
- Nurture your credibility.
- Publish an employee communication policy and communication guidelines for all managers.
- Use your personal communication style to advantage.

Step 2: Send your message

- Answer your employee's most common questions.
- Give employees the information they *need* to do their jobs.
- Seek and create opportunities to send messages.
- Give every internal communication a clear message for a well-defined purpose and audience. Deliver it through the best channel (including social networking technologies).

Step 3: Check for understanding

- Run employee surveys and engagement audits, talk with employee focus groups, get feedback data.
- Find out regularly if employees are receiving your intended messages.

External communication

7

- Introduction

- Step 1: Prepare yourself for external communication – 'the company'

- Step 2: Send your company message

- A final note on preparing yourself: recruiting a communications expert

Introduction

A member of the press speaks 'informally' with a manager of a company that makes sterilisation gel to combat the spread of the H1N1 virus. This manager, a scientist, notes correctly that the positive effects of the company's product have not yet been 'demonstrated conclusively' in clinical tests. The next day, a lead story in a British newspaper claims that the company is selling sterilisation gel that it knows is ineffective. It takes the communications team almost a week to recant the story and another week to portray the story accurately. But the damage is done.

Many global companies proclaim the value of integrated 'strategic' communications. Some get it right, but many do not. The ones who get it wrong lack a consistent strategy, or more specifically display a lack of effective strategy execution with communications not integrated through all parts of their worldwide operations.

As a company grows bigger and more complex – more markets, customers, products, services, employees, suppliers, investors and so on – it needs a consistent communication strategy, because it has to communicate to a diverse and rapidly growing audience where responsibility and decision-making authority have been dispersed.

Yet few companies communicate with external stakeholders as effectively as they could. They take a short-term approach to communicating with their key constituencies, with the focus on limiting financial or legal vulnerability. And many are still using approaches that worked in the 20th century, but are ineffective today.

It's time to take a strategic view of external communications: integrate it into your daily practice. Think strategically about your communication with all external stakeholders, remembering that everything you say outside the company walls 'can and will be held against you', especially in our day of instant MMS and video uploads to YouTube. For you, this means thinking about company communications in terms of the three-step communication model, modified to reflect the fact that the sender is the company itself, the messages need to be articulated by the relevant manager, coordinated among many people, over departments, approved by top management and then sent via the agreed channel. Usually you will not be sending official company messages, but you do send unofficial company messages every time you communicate. So you still need to prepare yourself and go through the steps of creating and sending clear messages. Checking for understanding is then the job, in most companies, of the communications, PR or marketing department. Nevertheless, all managers should take a keen interest in external communication effectiveness.

Step 1: Prepare yourself for external communication – 'the company'

Communicate as if you are the voice of the company

Everything about an organisation communicates messages. From product design to corporate culture and policies, media campaigns to press releases, company symbols to corporate charity – companies and their employees are communicating 24/7. The spread of new technology and the speed of business change have made corporate communications a front-line activity. A company sends messages even when it is silent.

Your company's shareholders, the media, governments and, most important, your customers are more impatient than ever to hear the latest 'official' company response to the company news of the moment, whether financial results, a merger or acquisition, new product release, safety recall, competitors' actions or executive misconduct. The company does not know when the next newsworthy event will break: but it will, and it will require a clear, consistent and confident statement regardless of who delivers the message. One day, *you* may be delivering that message.

Companies in which all managers are committed to effective external communication show higher shareholder returns (nearly 50 per cent higher in some cases) and greater market value (nearly 30 per cent greater) over time. External communications is now recognised as a valued strategic tool that plays a vital role in a company's total business system.

Your company may have an elegant business strategy, but if you fail to articulate it well, either inside the firm or to external stakeholders, you may be hurting your reputation, your brand, customer and media relations and perhaps even revenues. You're not alone: some companies outsource their communications functions, leaving a junior colleague in a 'coordination' role with no full-time member of the chief executive team to supervise. A vital part of strategy and strategy implementation is the communication of strategy: inside the company and out, upwards and downwards, and among all stakeholders. The dividing line between business strategy and communications strategy may be blurred, but effective communication is one of the keys to operations and execution, and a central part of setting strategy and executing it. Not only should you help implement strategy by communicating with your key constituencies, you should also help interpret the responses to inform your next business moves.

Communicate to enhance company position

It is your task is to help enhance your company's position and make sure that the business system runs smoothly, projects succeed and the company achieves its purpose, both in the short and long term. Create a role for yourself, even a small one, in company communications. Be one of the managers who cares about, and knows about, communication. Take every opportunity with external stakeholders to deliver the key company messages. Your company may require you to get media training before you speak with the media. Do it. Meantime, don't speak with a member of the media, give a phone interview or chat after an industry event. Most media training lasts a few days. It's fun, you'll learn a lot about your communication presence and style, and you'll be better prepared to communicate with any stakeholder.

The higher you sit on the company ladder, the more contact you have with outsiders who are interested in the fate of your company, the more you are under scrutiny. Curiosity is part of our nature – we want to hear the next, latest news, to get the next titbit of juicy information. Everything you say and write should be designed to get the desired response you want from the audience. Visualise external communication as a vast web, with your success as a communicator based on taking a long-term view. Your company needs a story, and you need to be able to tell it. All management communication in your company should be aligned and integrated. (All employees should know their company's story.) You may be rewarded for short-term, tactical success, but don't forget about long-term messaging.

Not making strategic communication a priority is a more of a problem than ever before because pressure on companies to provide fast, transparent information and responses is growing. Internet access is booming. Pressure groups wield more power than ever. Corporate complaint websites are cropping up every day. New blogs appear on the internet hourly. Corporate journalism dominates the media. Consumers are better informed and more involved. Unfortunately, for many managers communication is all about short-term action: 'We have a crisis? Let's deal with it!' Some will tell you that decisions about key communication issues in the company are reserved for the corporate communications team. Some companies even promulgate this view.

 Tip

If you don't respond to the growing pressure to communicate clearly and quickly, in one company voice, you will end up communicating reactively – a recipe for communication mishaps. This can hurt your brand and your reputation and may even hurt sales. So make your external stakeholder communications purposeful. Know your messages, and prepare and deliver them with a set purpose, to get a defined result.

As your company takes up the call to focus on value, and orients itself more towards customers, you need to know more about your customers and other stakeholders, and communicate more effectively with them. Your company's communications team may be working hard behind the scenes to deliver messages, all in one company 'voice'. But your company's messages may not be coordinated. Managers at every level feel as though they own the messages coming from their area of responsibility. Thus, your company's messages are anything but well coordinated – a mishmash of idiosyncratic messages that don't add up to a strong, clear company story.

What's in a name?

Products have failed overseas simply because a name may take on unanticipated meanings in translation: the Olympic copier Roto in Chile (*roto* in Spanish means 'broken'); the Chevy Nova in Puerto Rico (*no va* means 'doesn't go'); the Randan in Japan (*randan* means 'idiot'); Parker Pen's Jotter pen ('jockstrap' in some Latin American markets). This type of mishap is not an American monopoly. A successful European chocolate and fruit product was introduced into the US with the unfortunate name 'Zit'. Naming a product is external communication at its simplest level. The overall implications of external communication, in this case intercultural communication, for global business are enormous. These companies, it seems, paid little attention to the cultural context of communication. They didn't even check the meanings of the names of their products in their target markets. These are classic failures to think strategically about communication. If only such companies had asked the standard questions at the heart of any communication strategy:

- What is my communication (product naming) purpose?
- How can I best achieve it?
- Who is my target audience and how can I engage them?
- What is the communication context, the cultural mores and assumptions?
- What connotations do my words have for customers?
- What is my credibility, and how can I boost it with my communication, instead of undercutting it?

Integrate communication with strategy development and implementation

When many business strategy books mention communication, they usually zero in on organisation structure and processes, and the allocation of resources. The focus is often on *implementing* strategy – making sure that the strategy is broadcasted and works well, and that objectives are met. There is little talk about communicative processes and structures; to make matters worse communication books rarely cover managerial processes and structures.

When a management book touches on the role of corporate communications in strategic decision making, it is in the context of meeting largely tactical needs, for example, supporting marketing strategies. Or, corporate communications is seen as the communicator of business messages, rather than as the identifier and interpreter of key communications issues at the stage of strategy formulation.

We can learn lessons from companies where communications are aligned with company strategy and are fully integrated, even among widely dispersed offices and divisions. Credit Suisse, Shell, FedEx, Dell, PepsiCo, Tetra Pak, Compass Group and Securitas all involve their top communications people in strategy discussions, and communicate their strategy to varied constituents with the aim of getting them to 'buy in'. Their managers are involved in and committed to communications, and can align their own communications with the company's strategy and implementation.

To move beyond short-term approaches, all managers should help integrate communications in whatever way fits best, find ways to involve senior management, take a broad perspective, gain personal credibility, and make sure they have the skills needed to translate their part of the business into simple, clear messages that capture the company's vision, mission, strategy, value proposition, products, etc.

Attend to your external communications challenges

The process of external corporate communications has been likened to throwing a dart at a wall and then drawing a target around it. Audiences have more channels of information than ever before. Speed matters – information takes seconds to zoom around the globe. In some industries, companies have become synonymous with the personalities of their CEOs or top managers ('personalisation'). Think of Disney's Michael Eisner, Citigroup's Vikram Pandit, Apple's Steve Jobs, The Body Shop's Anita Roddick. Recently, Goldman Sachs was identified with its 'ethically challenged' young bond trader, Fabrice Tourre (known as Fabulous Fab), who testified in front of a US Senate panel about his role in the sub-prime meltdown. Nowadays, the CEO, some argue, represents 30–40 per cent of the image of a corporation.

Mistrust of balance sheets, auditors' reports and the ethical behaviour of corporations is growing. It is surmised that at GE, the combined personality of Jack Welch and the 'myth' around GE's supreme measurement culture, fostered by business-school case studies and articles in the press, kept an additional $2–3 on the company's share price. More than ever, the company 'personality' and targeted messages count. The challenge is to use external communications to turn a company's soft assets into hard assets.

Think and act like a chief communications officer

If you want to be a manager who communicates well outside the company, think of yourself as a the chief communications officer of your team, department, unit or division. My research into communications practices of senior managers revealed that the effective communicators did, indeed, think like strategic communications officers. They thought about their communication purpose, audience, context, messages, channels, timing – all the elements of a classic strategic communications plan.

Every company has a face and a story, and you're part of it. Your words, your actions, your behaviour, your attitude, even your clothes. You say something in a meeting, someone at the table records it on a phone, and next thing you know, it's in the hands of a reporter. You've just damaged your company's story.

> **Tip**
>
> **Remember: every person with a smartphone is a publisher and the truth will out. Whatever you do or say may end up on a website.**

Samantha was discussing a building project with her boss. Another employee dropped by to ask a question about the planning of the annual spring outing. Something about the size of the boat for a trip around the local lake. When the employee left, Samantha's boss said, 'That guy just doesn't get it. What an idiot.' What he didn't consider when he said this was that his door was open and his secretary of many years heard his remark. She later told a friend, who told a friend, and pretty soon, the story was lighting up the company's gossip circuits.

Worse, Samantha later had a call with a local journalist who asked her about the incident: 'Was it true that your boss had thrown a tantrum and threatened to fire an employee for booking the wrong bus?' he asked. Samantha had to explain the situation away and try to redirect the journalist's attention to 'more important matters'.

In April 2010, a hot business story has been the public grilling Goldman Sachs has taken at the hands of a US Senate subcommittee hearing. The bulk of the evidence against the Goldman managers are damning emails and SMSs they exchanged during the months they were both selling 'toxic mortgages' to unsuspecting investors and shorting those same instruments in-house. Whether their behaviour was legal or not, according to polls, many Americans viewed it as morally bankrupt. And the evidence is in the internal emails.

Appreciate your communications people – you may need them one day

In the past five years, I have asked more than 1,000 middle and upper-level managers what they think about their company communications people. More than 77 per cent doubt the value of the function, and more than 68 per cent suggest that the communications people spend their days 'writing press releases and making PowerPoint presentations for the CEO'.

Corporate (external and internal) communications is one of management's least appreciated, most complicated and most difficult jobs. It's hard to measure. Few newly-minted MBAs show much inclination to go into communications. It is rarely seen as critical to the success of the firm's business system. It is big, woolly, unwieldy, soft and often thankless. Communications experts are asked to manage the corporate brand, build identity, boost reputation and run communications. Some companies combine the various communications functions in one chief communications officer (CCO); others have a collection of top communications people, doing their best to work together formally or informally.

Company communications people need to know about change models and be able to run change communications. Good ones have broad general management skills and speak the same language as senior management. They should be good conceptual thinkers and strategic analysts. They must be good persuaders and have a deep understanding of the business and strategy garnered outside the communications function or in formal education (e.g. MBA, EMBA); possess business communications expertise – writing, editing, public speaking, templates, standards; know the tools of the trade; and have experience of crisis management, event management and media expertise.

The contractual tasks are many:

- orchestrate the company story
- message management
- media relations
- government relations
- employee and internal communications
- brand gatekeeper
- reputation manager
- investor relations
- financial, marketing and stakeholder communications
- corporate identity.

Communications people have the challenge of many jobs at once, and the balance of these jobs shifts daily. Unlike many managers, communications people have official or unofficial social roles: message framer; reputation barometer and manager; senior manager confidant; message seller and social conscience of the company. The role of top external communications people has been described as planner, watchdog, catalyst, communicator, savant, stimulant, strategic partner, coach, adviser and confidant. Specifically, they:

- React to crises, write press releases and prepare top management speeches and presentations.
- Work as editors and writers, even ghost writers.

- Monitor short-term legal and financial angles.
- Inform investors and financial editors.
- Serve as partners to top management, particularly the CEO, to ensure that communication practices contribute directly to the company's strategy implementation.
- Provide communication advice and information.
- Ensure that the company has a sustainable, harmonious 'story'.
- Help with risk management and damage control, keeping managers from saying the wrong things, especially in public.
- Communicate the big decisions about major company commitments.
- Diagnose which messages have to get to which ears, for which purposes, by which channels and in which vehicles, throughout the company and to key targets.
- Foster an online presence for company news both formally and informally. And going beyond the mere online presence, a company communications expert may be asked to oversee – or even create – a presence in the form of multiple profiles at popular social networking and blogging sites like Twitter, Facebook and LinkedIn, to name only a few in the rapidly changing world of electronic media.

Day-to-day, communications people spend their time on:

- press releases
- project planning
- interviews
- meetings
- memos
- newsletters
- conference calls
- events
- speeches
- philanthropy
- lobbying
- advertising.

At best, communications departments do a good job of conveying whatever management tells them to. They rarely take part in top management discussions; nor do they have much say in company strategy. They often fail to address the big picture – the business system and the ways the company creates value, the transformations required to link a company's priorities with those of its customers. All too often, company communications experts get caught up in short-term decisions and produce communications that are not strategic. No wonder – they are often rewarded for short-term, tactical performance, such as getting good media coverage, an excellent photo opportunity for the CEO, or running a smooth press conference. The chief communications officer has to cope with unexpected crises where instant media interest leaves little time for thinking.

The list of titles for top communications people is long. A look at the individuals who hold top communications jobs suggests that the responsibilities have been cobbled together around them, to match their skills and special abilities.

Company	Job title
Avon Rubber	Group Publicity Manager
British Airways	Director of Public Affairs
British Telecommunications	Director of Corporate Communications
GlaxoWellcome	Director of Group Public Affairs
Lloyds TSB	Head of Corporate Communications
W.H. Smith Group	Director of Corporate Affairs
Johnson & Johnson	VP, Public Affairs and Corporate Communications
FedEx	Executive Vice-President, Market Development and Corporate Communications
Dell	VP, Investor Relations and Corporate Communications
Coca-Cola	Director, Worldwide Public Affairs and Communications

Give communications people a place at the strategy table

Strategy discussion is richer and execution is improved in companies where the people who communicate strategy are also involved in its formulation. This involvement contributes to a clearer articulation of:

● company brand
● identity
● reputation
● messages
● a sustainable corporate story.

Your communications people can provide crucial input in major transactions such as mergers, acquisitions or restructurings. Ironically, they must make sure that communications isn't owned exclusively by the communications department, only that its messages appear well coordinated.

Tip

Remember: you can't implement strategy if you can't communicate it. And this is easier said than done.

Choose among the four external communication models

Four models have shaped external communications practice as it has evolved over decades from a selling tool to a dialogue with a company's most important stakeholders. Each model reflects a different degree of the power balance between the company and its stakeholders. This is key, since stakeholders arguably have more power than ever before. As company needs shift, and communications technologies and conventions change, the emphasis on one or the other model changes. Today, companies use all four models, and usually try to keep control of both the issues and the messages.

Propaganda model

The propaganda model, common in the 19th century, has the company manipulating the audience, using exaggeration and even direct falsehood. The propaganda approach shows a blatant disrespect for stakeholders' views. The company that chooses this model today often gets caught in a web of deceit. Think of Enron or, more recently, Goldman Sachs.

Public information model

This model gives stakeholders some respect. The company does not try to ignore or fool stakeholders, but the one-sidedness of the information prevents neutrality. Even with the best of intentions, the company effectively censors what it communicates – it rarely gives the whole story. Non-profit organisations and government agencies and businesses sometimes use this model.

Persuasion model

Users of this model aim to influence stakeholders by 'fair' means. Market surveys, for example, openly determine consumer needs and wishes. So long as the playing field is level, this is an effective, balanced approach. But persuaders usually know more about how to achieve their intentions than customers and stakeholders. This model is the preferred choice of most marketing departments.

Two-way model

The two-way external communication model aims to achieve mutual understanding and benefit. This is the model textbooks have heralded for decades, but it has been slow to catch on. No wonder: it starts with the premise of company and constituents being on an equal footing and engaging in dialogue. The problem is, a level playing field where company, customers and stakeholders engage in open dialogue is still a delusion.

Step 2: Send your company message

Take a lesson from company website communication

If your communication to external stakeholders comes across, to even one external stakeholder, as disingenuous, untruthful or confusing you may be hurting your company's reputation, brand or potentially its bottom line. If you're not on message and 'on pitch' you're not communicating well enough. The way you talk about your company says a lot about the company itself. You give a straight story; your top management colleague gives a pre-packaged, corporate communication message. These two divergent messages may make listeners wonder about the company's values, mission, goals and identity.

Take an example from websites, which are essentially the modern corporation's face to the world. Visit the websites of two companies that have been under some duress: Playtex and Johnson & Johnson. You'll find a number of digital communications that seem to be sending mixed messages. In each case, the company website may well cause visitors to ask themselves, 'What's going on here?' The question may reflect a breakdown of trust in the company's messages, and with it, slipping credibility.

If you visit www.playtex.com, there appear to be two identities. Playtex was once the company known for the Cross Your Heart Bra that could 'lift and separate'. In 1988, it was split into Playtex Apparel and Playtex Products.

But now, it seems, the two companies are not easily distinguishable, at least not on the web. The new names don't appear to say much about the different products or strategies. One could argue that even Playtex.com seems to struggle with the distinction: 'Although we may have a name in common… we are two completely separate companies.'

The separation may be complete, at least legally and within the organisation, but the two logos looks very much alike. The phrase 'completely separate' sounds somewhat strained, and suggests that perhaps the company knows consumers may have trouble telling the two apart. I would argue that it feels the need to clarify the difference, and this could lead to visitor distrust. Perhaps the introduction of a web redirect would offer a way to clarify any confusion between the identities of the two companies.

For many years, Johnson & Johnson (www.jnj.com) was admired in professional communications circles for the way it came back after the 1982 Chicago Tylenol murders. Its Tylenol website (www.tylenol.com) still projects self-assurance, in spite of January 2010 recalls of Tylenol, Rolaids, Motrin and Benadryl after complaints of a mouldy smell (*http://www.msnbc.msn.com/id/34877367/ns/health-more_health_news/*). *A big red button on the home page states 'Important Recall News' and links to a matter-of-fact press release and to a simple, convenient way to tell if you're holding a recalled Tylenol product. Tylenol positions its recall as though it was all in a day's work for a diligent company that manufactures many important products. It is up front about the recall, but it doesn't insist on trust, cast a cold eye on complaints or rail against its detractors.*

What's the management communication lesson in this web tour? Like managers' key messages, websites should be updated and speak the truth confidently or be shut down. If your plans, strategy or products change, make the change public on your website, and show confidence in your language and message online. If you get hit by a recall, your plans change or your performance drops, speak the truth. In this day and age, you will not be able to hide for long: the truth will out. So either you can try to control how it gets out, or you can let other news channels in the 24-hour news cycle run with it, change it, amplify it, and use it against you in ways you could never have imagined.

Be the company message

While the CEO is usually the designated spokesperson for the company, every manager is a *de facto* spokesperson for the company. The words you use become your company, and your company becomes the words its managers use. You need to 'be' the company message, to give it a positive personal touch. Your company products may not speak well for your company – think of the company Transoceanic, the world's largest offshore drilling company, whose semisubmersible drilling platform, Deepwater Horizon, exploded on 20 April, 2010, leaving nine people dead – but you can. Be consistent and credible in your position as a manager. You are, at least in small part, the living embodiment of your company. Right now, out there, a senior manager is leading the poorly performing division of some huge manufacturing company and doesn't realise that every time he opens his mouth in public, he is contributing to the downfall of his company, hurting its reputation, making it look – and sound – bad. After all, communication is about perception: it's not what you say, it's what people perceive. And in this case, they hear the mumbled platitudes of a man who just isn't careful enough about what he says.

Run change communication as a persuasive campaign

Communication is an important part of any successful change, whether it's a merger, acquisition, downsizing or reorganisation. Change initiatives require long-term persuasive campaigns. If you are managing change, you will usually have your hands full trying to run a multitude of change-related projects. But you will need to forge close ties between the change strategy and the communication strategy.

In any change effort, you will have to keep the channels of communication open. By the time senior management sets a direction, they may believe that communicating about it is not as important as making the actual changes. But it is precisely at this point that more open communication is needed to help implement the change and sell the ideas to those people not in the decision-making team. People have questions, worries, anxieties, and if they feel they are being heard or considered it is more likely they will stay aligned.

It is not enough for management to tell people about the planned changes in an email, often drafted by the CEO or someone in corporate communications. First, people need to know about the change, and then they need to understand the impact on their work. You must make sure that all communications to people affected by the change, both inside and outside the company, describe the rationale for the change, people's new roles, and the benefits that can be expected for employees, customers, shareholders, and the company. Of course, to manage this you'll need to have enough credibility to communicate change.

The five truths

When a crisis befalls your organisation – as no doubt, it will – you need to be prepared. Think about the mistakes Toyota made communicating during its wave of recalls in 2010. What truths should Toyota have ingrained into its communications processes? It could not have prevented the problems with its Prius, Camry and Corolla brake systems, but it could have done a better job communicating its response to those problems and the ensuing recalls.

Here are five truths you should bear in mind.

1 Communicate immediately

Organisations – or managers – that begin communicating immediately have a greater chance of becoming the media's primary go-to source for information during the crisis. Regular and open communication often leads to more balanced and sympathetic coverage. Communicating immediately doesn't make the bad stories go away, but it usually makes the stories shorter-lasting and less severe.

2 Slow communication worsens the crisis

If you don't respond to a crisis quickly, the media will get their information elsewhere. Outside sources are never as accurate, informed or measured as the organisation itself. When Ray LaHood, United States Secretary of Transportation, testified before Congress on 24 February, 2010 he said, 'My advice is, if anybody owns one of these [Toyota] vehicles, stop driving it.' That panicked Toyota investors, which drove down the stock price. LaHood later danced away from that comment, saying he had meant to say that his advice to people driving the vehicles would be, 'If you are in doubt, take it to the dealership today.' LaHood, speaking for the US Government, should have been a lot more careful with his words about the US auto industry. His gaffe was his own responsibility, but many acknowledge that Toyota allowed it to happen by issuing unclear guidance to government regulators and consumers.

3 Your response to a crisis changes the crisis

A company's initial response to a crisis changes the crisis itself. A brilliant crisis response will almost always lead to better (if not good) media coverage, whereas a lacklustre response almost always guarantees worse coverage. Early stories about Toyota's safety issues were focused on the cars themselves. But coverage quickly shifted to Toyota's poor handling of the crisis, compounding an already difficult story for the company. Its clumsy crisis response also created huge legal risks for Toyota. According to the wire service AFP, Toyota 'faces dozens of lawsuits in the United States alleging Toyota was too slow to act on the problems. Experts say the legal action could potentially cost the company billions of dollars.'

4 The media will focus on the victims

The media (and the public) tend to see crises from the perspective of the victims. A good crisis response puts victims first by demonstrating genuine concern and taking immediate action to protect their well-being. Toyota also failed on this count. According to the National Highway Traffic Safety Administration, almost three dozen people have died as a result of 'unintended acceleration' in Toyotas. But internal documents show that instead of protecting their customers, Toyota bragged to its board about saving money by initially limiting the recall.

5 Burying bad news rarely works

Trying to bury negative parts of the story often extends – and deepens – the crisis. The information usually gets out anyway, and the lack of forthrightness hardens any lingering suspicions about an organisation's integrity. After recalling more than eight million cars worldwide, Toyota announced in mid-February that it was also thinking about a recall of the Corolla for a problem related to steering. The bad news dripped out one drop at a time. How much more effective if Toyota had held a press conference announcing every problem they were aware of, as well as the specific solution they were putting in place for car owners? It would still have been a bad story for the company, but Toyota would probably have received some credit for its handling of the crisis.

Two tools for preparing and sending company messages

One of the world's largest mobile network providers was operating in a highly decentralised manner (this case has been disguised). Its communications departments were spread over five continents and six sectors. Each department said what it wanted, to whom it wanted, in the

way it saw fit. Because the company had grown mainly through acquisition, many of the country units were not well integrated into the parent company. Group discipline was lacking. There were contradictions in the company's image, key messages, branding guidelines and the investor news that the group was presenting to the outside world. Public relations initiatives were confusing employees, analysts, investors, journalists and customers alike. A new communications director was called in to integrate the communications functions into one entity that focused its first efforts on corporate branding and strategic communications objectives.

The new director standardised the structure and processes of the various communications functions. She hired heads of communication for each country, and made the department heads responsible for working closely with the communications officers. Frequent town halls were initiated, and the communications people met with the country heads once a month by video conference to agree key messages and communication strategies, especially when the company went through further reorganisation. The aim: to make sure the combined effect of all public relations activities around the world would portray a uniform, contradiction-free corporate story. Not only did this change make it possible for the new CCO and his team to coordinate communications for all target groups, which enhanced the group's international profile, but it also brought a reported 30 per cent reduction in communications costs.

When viewed overall, initially the company was sending fragmented, sometimes conflicting messages. Worse yet, it had no media relations policy, so managers often talked with local press, and their 'rogue' messages found their way into the international press. Many companies are aware of this danger, yet still fail to organise a coherent 'story'. Many of these inconsistencies could be ironed out if their communications experts could be involved earlier or had a stronger mandate and support. The strategic process is normally an ongoing, ever-changing blend of formal and informal interactions, and the communications experts need to be 'in the mix'. How else can they understand the strategy well enough to communicate it?

In many companies the output of communications specialists and managers results in a bricolage of messages – anything but a coherent story. To get strategic communications right, whether for an entire company, a division, unit or team, the challenges are the same: crafting a sustainable story, integrating all the communications that serve that story, building a communications plan to make it all happen and mastering the right personal skills to bring it all to fruition.

Tool 1: Create the company story

Companies have various ways of aligning communications. One practical approach is for all managers to view the company as having its own 'story'. We're not talking about a Hollywood account told for entertainment. We're not talking about a story with a plot, a report in a newspaper or a bit of gossip about the CEO or the delay of a new product. We're talking more about a story that captures the company strategy, brand, reputation, value proposition and customer promise.

The company story must convey originality or uniqueness; it is often built around the ideals of a great founder or a strong sense of purpose, business, social or otherwise. Think of Virgin's Richard Branson or easyJet's Stelios Haji-Ioannou, IKEA's Ingvar Kamprad or Dyson's James Dyson. Successful companies are distinguished by stories as idiosyncratic as they are. Companies that communicate well know their stories.

An effective manager knows the company story, can tell it and where necessary refine it. Knowing how to create this story and articulate it to others is a big step forward. But often, managers at all levels struggle to decide what exactly their story is. Even more difficult to define and control is the role of top management in creating and furthering the company story.

How can managers focus everybody in their team on the story that helps customers and employees understand, and be attracted to, the company? First, all communications with customers and other stakeholders need to be simple and clear (but not overly simple or general). No more strings of corporate 'bullshit'. No more hard sell, language neutered by abstractions and clichés, statements with no people behind them, obscure statements clouded by a fog of meaningless strings of words, no more boring stories and disingenuous testimonials. No more statements – from any manager – like this:

> After exhaustive analysis of the macroeconomic patterns and trends facing the company, we have come to the conclusion that a restructuring is profit-critical and vital to maintaining our position on the competitive landscape. A task force of senior executives and high potentials has been appointed to do reconnaissance on the issues and potential opportunities, and they will report back with a comprehensive analysis and implementation plan for the mission-vital changes necessary in transforming the company into a more agile, customer-centred enterprise.

This blather has nothing to do with a company story, or even effective communication. It is, in fact, corporate obfuscation – a cloud of word smoke. If you're seeking to develop your company story, you might need to revamp your communications function. You will certainly have to make managers responsible for communication. You may have a list of 'core competencies' that describes the skills required of managers. It may include phrases like 'communicates effectively, clearly and frequently with employees'. Not one example I've seen defines effective communication in detail. None requires managers to know the company story, which won't take hold unless all top executives and mid-managers are telling it.

The difficulty of the switch to more strategic communication implied by the company story should not be underestimated. Anyone who has tried to make a clear, engaging presentation, and have the message stand over time, knows this. Creating the company story cannot be entrusted solely to the communications department, as much as many managers would wish it so. The key messages that make up the story need to reflect company strategy, so top management must go through an exercise of asking the right questions.

Achieving clarity in all the elements of a story requires intense debate. So, top management must be involved. They will have to explain the story to the people who work for them, usually other managers, so the story can ripple on down the chain. Every employee should be able to tell at least a simple version of the company story. I once asked more than 400 staff of a leading business school to describe the school's business model and objectives, product and market choices, its identity in the marketplace, and reputation. Only a handful came up with half-way coherent answers. Only a small minority could explain why customers would pay high fees to attend its programmes.

For a company story to take hold, the process must never be a one-off. It must be consistent over time, part of the company's regular marketing communications work (internally and externally). It needs to be honed, refined and strengthened, repeated often but not overused. It certainly needs the support of the CEO and other senior managers. The story-building exercise should be built into the regular strategy-setting exercises and marketing planning cycles. Revising it, with changes in the key messages, should become part of all strategic plans.

Topic	Questions to ask
Strategy	1 Does everybody in the company understand the business model and objectives? 2 How can we make sense of and describe what we're doing day-to-day? 3 Can we describe the business model so that both employees and customers can understand it?
Positioning	4 What are our product and market choices? 5 How will we articulate them? 6 Have we considered all key stakeholders?
Identity: actual and desired	7 What is the identity of our company to internal and external stakeholders? (The CCO must be familiar with the many measurement tools available.) 8 What influence do certain aspects of our identity have on our performance? 9 To what degree have all constituent parts of the company agreed on our key messages?
Reputation	10 What is the reputation of our company? 11 How will we measure our reputation? 12 What is the influence or correlation of reputation (positive or negative) on our performance? 13 What factors influence our reputation most strongly and how can we improve?

Brand	14 What is our brand? What is its added value?
	15 How can I orchestrate our internal decision making with an endorsement of the corporate brand at the business unit level?
Company story: write revise validate	16 What are the key promises that our company makes?
	17 What support will 'prove' these claims?
	18 What are our most important messages?
	19 In what 'tone of voice' will we tell our story?
	20 How compelling is our story?
	21 How well does it capture our identity, reputation, brand and messages?
	22 Have we involved top management, marketing, human resources, and communications?
	23 Does everybody inside the company know the story, share it, and believe in it?
Implement final version	24 How will we apply the story to all forms of communication?
	25 Who must be involved for the story to get out?
	26 Who will be the gatekeeper of the story?
Monitor	27 How will we measure whether our story works?
	28 How will we recognise success?
	29 How often will we revisit our story?

Tool 2: Create an integrated strategic communications plan

Managers are not responsible for articulating the company story. That's the CEO's and Chief Communication Officer's job. The CCO of your company, if you have one, is the *chief* message integrator. He or she defines the company's various communications and their objectives, delineates the primary and secondary target constituencies, and chooses the channels. But getting the story, with all its messages, across to everyone who works for you, is *your* job. You are the chief message integrator and company storyteller in your area. A useful way to think about this task is to use the following functional integration matrix.

Communication functions	Objectives	Target stakeholders (primary)	Target stakeholders (secondary)	Channels and communicators
Media relations	Public relations; crisis management	Media	All constituencies	Press releases, interviews: COO/CFO/CEO Corp. Comms; PR team; media relations team
Employee relations	Internal consensus building; engagement; drive change	Employees	Customers NGOs	Town hall meetings, memos, newsletters, video, webcasts, conference calls, web logs (blogs) CEO, HR, CCO; Corp Comms.
Financial communications	Transparency; meeting financial expectations	Investors	Analysts Media	Conference calls Press conferences: CEO, CFO, CCO
Community relations	External; image building; reputation enhancement	Communities	NGOs Media	Events; speeches; philanthropy CEO, CCO; top management
Government relations	Regulatory compliance; meeting social expectations	Regulators	Media Customers	Lobbying efforts One-on-one meetings CCO, CEO, CFO, government affairs officer; PR
Marketing communications	Driving sales; building image	Customers	All key constituencies	Advertising Promotions: marketing, advertising
Stakeholder communications	Image building; meeting expectations	Main stakeholders	Secondary stakeholders	Main stakeholders CEO, CFO, COO, Corp. Comms; PR
Competitor communications	Information sharing	Competitors	Customers of competitors	Press releases Media collateral

Once top management has drawn up and integrated the communications functions, they will need to draw up strategic plans for any major company change or initiatives, whether mergers, acquisitions, redundancies, divestitures, etc. When the communications strategy is unclear (or unarticulated), the communications plan is poor, and the results will be unclear roles, insufficient follow-up and mixed messages to stakeholders. Or worse, the corporate communications plan will be ignored and each major functional area will build their own. This was the case in our unfortunate, fictitious mobile network provider on page 127.

Once the story is clear to all, the communications people in your company need to put together a strategic communications plan. It's another matrix that looks much like the example overleaf.

The plan is a living document, since it essentially frames all media activities, including all internal and external communications, but it also clarifies the company's strategic priorities, target constituencies, resources and communications assignments.

The big, hairy challenge of a communications plan is execution. This is obvious when you have a major change, bad or unplanned news coverage, or a merger to manage. The difficulty is not so much articulating the purpose, messages, audiences and channels. Most people in a business can fill in the cells of a spreadsheet and agree on the plan. They can usually agree on who does what, who says what and how, and how things will be done. And then getting them all done. But the problem is that someone has to actually write the messages and get them out through the agreed channels. Especially in large, widely dispersed departments, this is a long, winding road, with pot holes and obstructions. It demands perseverance and energy, and an uncommon attention to detail: an almost neurotic degree of follow-up. All too many communications plans, like many large projects, never reach fruition.

To execute the plan, the CCO obviously needs to understand the company mission and vision, values and beliefs, and strategic goals. These elements must inform or shape every communication decision. But creating and executing such a plan requires that the CCO and the communications team get critical elements right:

- Know each target audience, internal or external, and how to reach it.
- Have research into past communications to these audiences.
- Articulate the messages to be delivered.
- Clearly define the materials to be produced.
- Get the resources.
- Have a written project management plan, including a crisis control plan and an evaluation or 'after action review' aspect.

Audience/target	Purpose	Key messages	Vehicles	Timing: when/how often	Responsibility: who from
Middle managers	Buy-in Understanding Dialogue New skills	New roles New methods Personal impacts	Meetings: CEO and senior management Training	Launch: week 1 Then weekly	CEO Senior managers Training department
Employees	Buy-in Understanding Dialogue New skills	New roles New methods Personal impact	Meetings with managers; intranet; training	Launch: week 1 Then weekly and daily	Managers Training department HR Internal Communications
Customers	Information Awareness	New methods, products, services, interfaces Service impact	Meetings with sales reps; newsletters; email blasts; customer web portals	Launch: week 1 Monthly	Managers Training managers
Shareholders	Information Awareness Support (votes)	Service impact Financial impact	Written information from CEO and CFO	Launch: week 1 Quarterly	CEO and CFO Head of board
Community	Information Awareness	Service impact Financial impact	Press releases	Launch: week 1 Define frequency	CEO; PR; Corporate Communications; Community Relations

A final note on preparing yourself: recruiting a communications expert

Today's communications professionals need to oversee the formulation of messages, set up the delivery channels, create the opportunities for communication, and conduct events. They need to understand the nuts and bolts of the company's business well enough to take part in the conversation. Gone are the days when the communications person could be merely an accomplished communicator – today's business challenges are far too complex. For example, the communications person working in a private bank does not need to be an ex-trader, an expert on collateralised debt or ultra-high net worth individuals, but understanding the concerns and challenges of private bankers and their clients will improve the company's communications. Managers would be well-advised to pick up or hone many of the skills communications professionals require:

- strategic thinking
- analysis and problem-solving skills
- ability to grasp business issues quickly and explain them to stakeholders
- communications practice
- public speaking, presentation and writing skills
- research skills
- meetings skills
- change management skills, including the psychology of change
- project management
- web design and measurement
- electronic media and social networking
- influencing skills
- coaching and mentoring skills.

 *Briefing Lessons*

To communicate with external stakeholders, every company – and all its managers – should adopt a long-term communication strategy and follow the three-step communication model, only on a large scale, as follows:

Step 1: Prepare for external communication

- Articulate three to five key messages and always stay on message.
- Integrate communication with strategy development and implementation.
- Let the communications people advise you.
- To understand what may work with certain stakeholders, be aware of common external communication models: the propaganda model, public information model, persuasion model, two-way model.

Step 2: Send the company messages

Creating and sending consistent, targeted messages is hard enough when all is going well, but in a crisis communication is doubly difficult, and mistakes are amplified.

- In a crisis, communicate immediately: slow communication worsens a crisis.
- Your response to a crisis changes the crisis.
- Media and other stakeholders often focus on the victims.
- Burying bad news rarely works.
- Use two tools to prepare company communication: the company story; and an integrated strategic communications plan.

Step 3: Check for understanding

This step involves measuring the impact of company external communication, and is covered in the next chapter.

How to measure management communication

8

- Checking for understanding on a large scale

Checking for understanding on a large scale

Do you measure the effectiveness of your employee and external communications? If not, why not?

Think of measuring the impact of your communications as a way to uncover problems that you can turn into opportunities for improvement. A weak, muddled communication can be a chance to create sharper, better targeted communications. Your measurement exercise – think of it as business research – will be a series of steps that you design with one goal in mind: resolving communications problems, whether personal, internal or external. The first step in fixing any communication problem is finding out exactly where it exists in the organisation and to identify as precisely as possible the communications problems and opportunities you need to study and resolve. Once you've defined the problem, you can take steps to gather information, analyse the data, determine the factors associated with the problem or opportunity (perhaps, the causes), and take the necessary actions to solve the problem or exploit the opportunity.

The difference between the manager who uses 'common sense' and 'hunches' or 'gut instincts' and the manager who uses a more scientific method is that the second one makes a systematic inquiry using data collected for scientific purposes (even if that data is qualitative). The manager who does this systematically, critically, diligently, objectively and logically stands a far better chance of improving communications. What better argument for measurement than this one?

Measuring your interpersonal communication effectiveness is a matter of checking for understanding, the third step in the three-step communication model. You simply determine the gap between your intended message and what the audience understood your message to be – by asking directly, paraphrasing, active listening, or through regular, open dialogue. The smaller the gap, the more effective the communication. But how do you measure your communication with groups of employees or other internal and external stakeholders? In terms of our three-step communication model, the question is: how do you determine whether groups of stakeholders have understood your message?

What you need to measure

Despite the apparent need for hard proof of communication value, the majority of managers and people in communications functions still plump for 'soft' measures. So what can you measure to get harder proof?

- The impact of communications activities and the extent to which they changed behaviour, skills and understanding. This is vital during change programmes.
- Your communication with your line managers and other stakeholders.
- The quality of executive and manager communication (including upward and peer feedback to executives and managers), both inside the company and outside.

- The extent to which employees and other important stakeholders believe that you support them.
- How well you inform employees and outside stakeholders of external issues.

There is a big difference among employees between being interested in a topic and being well informed about it. There are methods for checking this. Employees trust different sources of information and prefer different channels and media for different topics. For example, if they don't trust what the CEO says, they may try to get information from his deputy, or even his secretary. So you should check different stakeholder groups. Bottom line: every organisation is different, so you'll have to do your own breakdown of key factors to measure.

Two salient communication measurement questions

1 What communication do we measure?
2 How do we measure that communication?

You need to know how much value your communication is providing in terms of the economies of scale achieved and the degree (or success) of the communication – your ability to influence the quality of communication throughout the organisation.

You should measure the extent to which your communications experts are involved and consulted (for example, in the face of an oncoming crisis) and note how many executives and managers seek their advice, expertise and know-how.

You should be looking at how effectively your communications are coordinated to achieve economies of scale across business units and in various locations. Try to track savings through economies of scale by calculating savings from coordination and comparing costs to other similar organisations.

Further, you should be overseeing the quality of corporate internal communications and taking all necessary actions to ensure that they are effective. You should have access to the results of communications audits: benchmark them against the relevant norms, 360-degree feedback and upward feedback on communications ratings (these should compare managers).

When you measure communication, you need to distinguish between your measures of the effectiveness of your organisation's communication and what your employees think of your organisation's communication. You're unlikely to meet your organisation's communication objectives if you don't satisfy your employees' communication needs. You measure this in three ways: quantitative research, qualitative research or a mixture of both, which probably gives you the most accurate picture.

Quantitative research

Quantitative research measures simple things by survey. You can ask straightforward questions, like:

- Did employees receive, attend, read, review or listen?
- Did they understand it (you can test their knowledge and recall)?
- Did they like it?
- Did it add value?
- Did they change?

Typical quantitative approaches to communication measurement

Simple surveys	Quick completion forms or emails
	Telephone and quick interview polls
Special instruments	360-degree feedback surveys
	Surveys on communication effectiveness
Comprehensive questionnaires	Employee opinion surveys
	Communication audits
	Values surveys
Electronic group surveys	Groups

Advantages of quantitative communication measurement

Quantitative research offers a number of advantages. You can:

- Measure strengths and weaknesses by area.
- Determine what is working well and what isn't.
- Monitor trends over time to determine where your communications are more or less effective.
- Compare your organisation to others.
- Possibly find statistical correlations of employee satisfaction. For example, you may be able to determine the main drivers of employee commitment.
- Measure, in a limited way, culture, climate or the values in use.

In addition, you obtain the following advantages:

- You get relatively precise measurements (classifications, levels, service, gender, etc.).
- You can reach all employees, through a census for example.
- You can track progress over time and compare this to national and industry norms.

- You may be able to get 'predictive' correlations (key drivers) in order to indicate the relative importance and priorities.
- It is easy to give feedback to employees.

Disadvantages of quantitative communication measurement

The quantitative research method is not a panacea – there are disadvantages:

- The very items you choose will 'bias' your findings (I suggest you do qualitative research first to identify which issues to cover).
- The response rate can sometimes be a problem. You should be aiming for 95 per cent confidence for all categories.
- In small organisations, it can be costly per-person. You need to be careful what you cover, as employees may overestimate their level of knowledge.
- It is hard to cover complex issues with accuracy.
- You don't find out why things are the way they are.

Challenges of quantitative communication measurement

There are, of course, special challenges to quantitative research:

- You need an experienced survey designer.
- You need some qualitative research to start with.
- You need to take extreme care with questions and demographics.
- You need multiple measures for each 'construct', as employees may fear identification by their manager if they provide 'negative' answers.
- You may have to remind people or even schedule 'completion' sessions.

When to use quantitative measurement

Given all this complication, I recommend you use quantitative research when you know the issues (say, lack of clarity about company strategy), but want to assess magnitude. You need numbers to convince your boss. You want to assess progress over time (by area). You need to measure strengths and weaknesses and are curious enough to look at benchmarks among competitors, and best practice firms in your industry, region, etc. You may have many locations or job classifications and you therefore may not be able to get staff for effective focus groups.

Typical qualitative measurement approaches

With qualitative research, you can investigate complex issues through interviews, focus groups, phone calls (asking open questions):

- What did employees think in detail?
- How much did they trust the source? Why?
- What more needs to be done for them to change their views or their behaviours?
- What questions, concerns or issues do they have?
- What are their expectations?

Say you want to know employees' thoughts and feelings, their suggestions, or reactions to your communication programmes. Qualitative approaches to measuring communications include:

- individual in-depth interviews, in person or on the telephone
- focus groups, either as a stand-alone, or combined with a survey, where you run them before or after the survey to discuss the findings
- asking for written comments both free response and open ended. (You can build such things into your questionnaires or create email response forms with response boxes. You've probably seen such comment boxes on hotel questionnaires.)
- 'quick polling', where you ask employees at the coffee machine, in the company restaurant or even in the parking lot.

You need at least 60 people in a random sample to pick up more than just the most common views:

- You'll need a simple comments form (print and online).
- You'll need 5–6 focus groups.
- You'll need three people to run telephone interviews with 20 people each from your sample (be sure that the interviewers ask the same questions in the same order).
- You can do a combination of these.
- For the research itself, you'll need a project team to help you conduct the research and, more importantly, to do the analysis.

Advantages of qualitative communication measurement

Qualitative research can reveal the reasons for gaps, the background, people's thoughts and feelings, the details and stories, and the rich narratives of their experience. With qualitative research, you can:

- Find out the overall concerns of your employees, unbiased by the questions you ask (or don't ask).
- Explore complex issues in considerable depth (e.g. how do employees trust the company on certain subjects, or what rumours are they believing).
- Get details of and reasons for many problems (with rich examples, evidence, where and when, and also get ideas).
- Get a highly 'granular' and detailed assessment of your company culture, climate and values (and the differences between what you want and expect, and the reality).

This kind of research is easy to organise and you don't need a long lead time. Compared to questionnaires, it may be cheaper – so long as you can reach the interviewees in the location of choice.

Disadvantages of qualitative communication measurement research

- You can't get precise measurements and, if you have many locations and functions, it's difficult to get a good representation.
- In some organisations, it may be difficult to run focus groups and long, in-depth interviews. One interview can last up to 90 minutes. Only in a very small organisation can you afford to conduct qualitative research of everyone.
- The quality of the results depends heavily on the research skills in interviewing and in analysing the results.
- The results themselves can be long and bulky. If you transcribe interviews, you can easily end up with hundreds of pages for a few interviews. In a qualitative piece of research I did on strategic storytelling in a large, international organisation, my 60 interviews generated more than 1,500 pages of transcript results. Analysing them required much time and patience.

Challenges of qualitative communication measurement

The biggest challenges of qualitative research include:

- The need to do interviews in small groups and on sensitive subjects.
- The need for an experienced facilitator and analyst.
- The need to segment your population into groups.
- Focus groups and interviews can become 'griping sessions' (which can generate good ideas, but may raise expectations falsely and provide little more than mean-spirited gossip).
- It can be hard to group messy findings into clear, simple concepts and useful findings.

- Your boss may not find the research 'scientific' enough.
- It may be costly in time and effort to type up, sort and analyse the data (which comprises words, and more words).

When to use qualitative measurement

Use qualitative research to find out about overall workforce patterns; when you have complex issues to explore (many communications issues are, indeed, complex); to discover why you have problems; when you have many employees in few locations and have relatively few job classifications; and when you need the results fast and are on a limited budget.

Combine the best of both methods

From experience, I strongly recommend a combination of both qualitative and quantitative research. Here are some simple steps in such an approach:

1 Identify key communications issues with focus groups or a simple audit.
2 Cover key issues well: run a census questionnaire.
3 Make predictive correlations to identify priorities.
4 Conduct more focus groups in best and worst areas.
5 Seek 'understanding' of numbers in groups.
6 Cover sensitive or complex issues in groups.
7 Discuss improvement ideas in focus groups.
8 Process findings in work teams and plan your actions.

Briefing Lessons

You can measure the impact of your communication by doing scientific research. Two key questions are:

1 What communication do we measure?
2 How do we measure it?

There are two major communication research methods:

1 **Quantitative research:** measures the communication impact using surveys, special instruments (like 360-degree feedback), opinion surveys, audits and electronic group surveys.
2 **Qualitative research:** investigates complex issues through in-depth interviews and focus groups, written comments and quick 'informal' polling.

Each method has advantages and disadvantages. The main ones are:

Quantitative research

- **Advantages:** relatively precise measurements; large samples; predictive correlations possible.
- **Disadvantages:** the items you choose to research are likely to bias your findings; low response rates; may be expensive; does not cover complex issues well.

Qualitative research

- **Advantages:** find out overall concerns, opinions and views of a group; explore complex issues in depth; get details and reasons.
- **Disadvantages:** precise measurements are unavailable; can be time-consuming; quality depends on the skills of the interviewer; results can be long, bulky documents.

How to talk about management communication

9

The following is an expanded glossary of the key communication terms and concepts you will need to be familiar with in your communications role.

Blog (web log)

A blog is a website where entries are made in journal style and displayed in reverse chronological order. The term 'blog' is derived from 'web log'. 'Blog' can also be used as a verb, meaning *to maintain or add content to a blog.* Blogs often provide commentary or news on a particular subject, such as food, politics or local news; some are like personal online diaries.

Communications plan(-ning)

Communications planning (creating a communications plan) is about figuring out how to communicate important messages to an organisation's key stakeholders effectively. Communications plans may focus internally or externally. Elements of communications planning include: communicating the company vision, philosophy and information. Key concerns of communications planners are credibility, key messages, channel, audience, timing and effectiveness.

Communication process

Communication is a process in which information is enclosed in a package and channelled and imparted by a sender to a receiver via some medium. The receiver then decodes the message and gives the sender feedback. All forms of communication require a sender, a message, and an intended recipient. However, the receiver need not be present or aware of the sender's intent to communicate at the time of communication in order for the act of communication to occur. There are auditory means (speech, tone of voice, song) and there are non-verbal means (body language, sign language, paralanguage, touch, eye contact) and media (pictures, graphics, sound and writing).

Corporate communications

Corporate communications is the orchestration of all the elements of a company's identity to create a competitive advantage. Corporate communications can involve management communication, organisational communication and marketing communication. It thus means facilitating information and knowledge exchanges with internal and external groups and individuals that have a direct relationship with an enterprise.

Channel

The mode by which or through which a message is transmitted from sender to receiver. Examples are face-to-face conversations, presentations, meetings, email blasts, corporate websites, newsletters, webcasts, podcasts, memos, tweets and social networking sites.

Company story

The commonly agreed-upon story that colours and shapes all forms of a corporation's communication. Corporate stories increase the distinguishing power of a company, simplify the orchestration of communication and build a story through the common efforts of top management and the human resources, marketing and communications departments.

Electronic media

Electronic media refers to one or more of the following. The transition of websites from isolated information silos to sources of content, functionality, conversations and feeds, and even web-based software applications. Electronic media embraces, generates and distributes web content itself, characterised by open communication, decentralisation of authority, freedom to share and reuse, and 'the market as a conversation'.

Employee communications

Employee communications includes all communication inside an organisation. It may be informal or a formal function or department that provides communication in various forms to employees. The 'products' of internal communication can include intranets, newsletters, emails, blogs and surveys.

Encoding and decoding

Encoding is the process of transforming information from one format into another, usually words, images, sounds, gestures and facial expressions. The opposite operation is called decoding.

File transfer protocol (FTP)

File transfer protocol is a standard network protocol used to copy a file from one host computer to another, most commonly over the internet. A network protocol is a formal description of the formats of messages and the technical rules for exchanging those messages.

Message

The information sent by the sender and received by the destination (receiver).

Receiver

The person who receives or 'consumes' the message.

Sender

The source of a message.

Social networking site

A social network is a social structure made up of nodes that are generally individuals or groups connected through various social familiarities ranging from casual acquaintance to close familial bonds. Social networks operate on many levels, from families up to the level of nations. A social networking site is one of many internet applications to help connect friends, business partners or other individuals together using a variety of tools. Examples include Facebook, Twitter, LinkedIn, FriendFeed, Delicious, Flickr.

Stakeholders

The word 'stakeholder' as used in management means a person or organisation that has a legitimate interest in a company, its performance, products or issues. Stakeholders typically include vendors, employees and customers, but even members of a community where its offices or factory may affect the local economy or environment.

Wiki

A wiki is a website that allows collaborative editing of its content and structure by its users. Many companies use them as platforms for employee collaboration. A good example is 'Wikipedia' (www.wikipedia.org).

[PART THREE]

Intervention

Executive intervention

10

- What are my make or break decisions?

- When is my intervention needed?

- What questions should I ask and whom should I ask?

- What levers should I pull?

- How do we know when we've succeeded or failed?

What are my make or break decisions?

The make or break decisions in communications are related to the choices you make in each step of the three-step communication model. You make these crucial decisions many times every day – each time you communicate at work. Don't fall into the trap of thinking that any communication is insignificant. You can never know the ramifications of poor communication. So, the first make or break decision is how much you will commit yourself to improving your communication. Once you make the commitment, you then need to take a long-term strategic communication path. Think of each communication as three interconnected steps: preparation, sending the message and checking for understanding (measuring). You then need to create a portfolio of key messages for each important stakeholder group (this may actually be one person, like your CEO) that will help move your company toward its goals. That way, you will avoid the most common pitfalls of short-term, reactive communication.

Make or break interpersonal communication decisions

- How important is communication to me?
- How do I want to be perceived as a communicator? What do I want employees to say about my communication practices?
- How will my communication boost morale, and improve individual and team performance?
- What percentage of my time will I choose to spend on communication?
- How I will take advantage of my communication style, and also get myself to a place where my weaknesses are less of a handicap?
- How will my communication best benefit the company?
- Which people will I treat as top priority stakeholders and how will I communicate with them accordingly?
- Who are the key influencers in the organisation and how can I best communicate with them?
- What is my personal communications plan? What are my communication objectives and how do they directly benefit the business?
- What are my personal 3–5 key messages?
- How often will I meet with employees?
- How will I create an atmosphere of open dialogue and trust among my colleagues?
- How will I measure the effectiveness of my own communication?

Make or break employee communication decisions

- How will we, as a company, communicate with our employees?
- How we will measure employee engagement and satisfaction and its correlation with our internal communication?
- How can we ensure that we have employee communications policies in place that will help the company meet its targets?
- How can we make effective communications a part of management and employee performance criteria?
- How will we measure the effectiveness of our employee communication?
- What do we expect from managers and employees in their communications with one another?
- How will I communicate to build employee satisfaction and boost performance?
- How can we ensure that our employee communication during major change initiatives is a purposeful, persuasion campaign?
- How can I most effectively communicate the key results and expectations so that there is no ambiguity among employees? This includes answering the five key employee questions:
    - What's my job?
    - How am I doing?
    - Does anyone care?
    - How are we doing?
    - What is our company vision, mission and values?

Make or break external communication decisions

- How will we communicate to build customer and employee satisfaction?
- How effective is our web presence? What can we do to improve it?
- How will company communication help keep our products and services at the top of the market?
- How can we be prepared for a crisis, especially in our communications response?
- How will we build a sustainable company story?
- How will we communicate to build our brand and reputation?
- How will we communicate our vision and mission?
- How will we measure the effectiveness of our external communications strategy and tactics?

When is my intervention needed?

If you observe any of the following symptoms, your intervention to improve communication may be needed:

- low employee morale or engagement
- low trust, high doubt
- loss of talented employees
- high churn rate among employees
- poor performance
- sabotaged careers
- low-performing virtual teams
- mobbing
- missed business targets
- bottlenecks in company processes
- failed change projects
- lack of clear direction
- vague vision, no sense of mission
- confused stakeholders
- a poor company reputation
- dropping sales
- disgruntled investors
- disillusioned customers
- bad news in the media, especially on the internet.

These symptoms (only a sample of many) signal that you need to investigate your communications practices. You probably need to review your long-term communications strategy, from the company's external communication right on down to the interpersonal interactions among people. Your intervention first takes the form of exploring – measuring – the effectiveness of all the communications in your area of the business. Interventions in company communications involve every tool presented thus far. There is no single intervention, no recipe for improving communication, so the best advice is this: when you've got a communication problem, you need to start your intervention by measuring using quantitative, qualitative or mixed-methods research. Generally, your research data will reveal to you the most effective intervention.

Intervention in the personal communication sphere

On an interpersonal level, you need to intervene if your employees aren't performing up to the standard you set, since poor communication may be at fault. It may be that you don't need to find ways to motivate your employees, but rather to stop demotivating them. You may need to revise policies and procedures, but also repair broken relationships. Remember, the majority of employees want to:

- feel respected and treated fairly
- feel pride in their jobs, achievements and their employer
- build good, productive relationships with their workplace colleagues.

Even if you're responsible for a small team, you can intervene by improving your everyday communication practice. You can't control top management decisions or rewrite company policy, but a small communications intervention can build employee motivation dramatically. To do this, you need to:

- Communicate a deep, abiding sense of purpose.
- Recognise people for good work, small and large.
- Tell your employees that you are not there to bark commands, but to help them get their jobs done.
- Make every conversation with employees a coaching opportunity. Give them relevant feedback on performance, listen actively, follow up and create dialogue. Practise regular communication.
- Give employees all the information they need. For this, you'll have to listen. And counter their natural scepticism by providing information straight up.
- 'Put the fish on the table': face up to conflict and poor performance. Deal with the low performers openly.
- Build self-managed teams and give them clear objectives. Make sure team communication boosts camaraderie.
- Listen and involve. Become a participative communicator.
- Teach your employees and colleagues the three-step communication model so it becomes ingrained in company communication culture, practices and processes.

Determine the general effectiveness of internal communications

Another vital intervention, if you see any of these symptoms or even suspect them, is measurement. Once you've defined a gap by measuring for it, you can design a plan (intervention) to close the gap. You'll need to measure the effectiveness of your own and the company's communication, the impact of it on your processes and infrastructure, and specifically how any of your company's communication programmes support company goals by:

- changing behaviour
- reinforcing existing effective or sanctioned behaviours
- increasing knowledge, sharing knowledge and building understanding
- reinforcing company values and desired culture.

To measure leadership or your own management communication, you can take any of the following measures:

- general 360-degree feedback or other widely used feedback systems (this may focus purely on communication)
- employee opinion surveys and communications audits (by survey or focus groups)
- observation of your own performance or that of other executives and senior managers:
  - How and where do they spend their time communicating?
  - How often do executives engage with employees?
  - What do managers say and to whom? When?
  - Are messages consistent? Simple? Logical? Relevant?

Determine the effectiveness of company communication processes

Before you intervene in the company structure in order to improve communication – with a reorganisation, reshuffling of key people, or new hires, for example – you need to assess the meaning and effectiveness of the company infrastructure by asking questions like the ones in the list below.

- What is the meaning that employees and other stakeholders get from such things as policies, procedures, systems and processes?
- Management reporting: who reports and what gets measured? What messages do budgets and project funding systems reinforce?
- Remuneration and recognition: who gets what? Why? What is honoured and rewarded? Who is more likely to get promoted and why? What behaviours and performance are rewarded?
- Organisation structure: what does the structure of the company say about who and what is important?
- Company 'story': what is the perceived company story? What are its missions, values, strategy, etc.? And what communications contribute to those aspects?

> As effective communication is situational, so every company will get differ-ent answers to the above questions. There is no one golden intervention, but the first step in any effective intervention is to define the gaps between the current state of communication and your desired state.

Another communication intervention is measuring the effectiveness of your company's communication programmes so you can start in on the necessary improvement. However, what you measure will depend on communications objectives for the company's various programmes. You may have any number of common communication purposes:

- to change behaviour or the way things get done
- to reinforce appropriate and productive behaviour
- to change attitudes or opinions about something
- to increase knowledge or understanding
- to raise general awareness or inform the audience.

You need to measure whatever the organisation expects of you, your corporate function and what your employees expect of you. As for 'how' to measure, you can use quantitative research, qualitative research, employee preferred content and sources and channels/media for various content. Basically, you need a way to measure what (if any) changes can be attributed to your company's communi-cation programme(s). You need to check if you or your communications people are doing a good job. One way is to measure behaviour, skills and knowledge before and after you communicate to determine changes (if any). Or you can use a 'control' group that does not get the communication. This entails measuring in control and experimental groups before and after the communication.

There are many possible measures, but among the most common in compa-nies are:

- enquiry rates
- calls made
- sales
- orders
- production
- reject rates
- transactions
- staff turnover
- performance appraisal and 360-degree ratings instruments
- employee and company culture surveys
- cost per transaction, call, etc.

What questions should I ask, and whom should I ask?

For every one of the three spheres of communication – the interpersonal sphere, employee communication sphere and external communication sphere – you need to answer a few pivotal questions if you are to adhere to the strategic, three-step communication model. In some cases, you will be asking these of yourself, as part of your preparation. In other cases, you will be checking on the understanding of the receivers of your messages, whether inside or outside the company.

Key questions for every communication

Message tool

Purpose of communication	1 Why are you doing this?
	2 What do you want to achieve?
	3 Does the purpose support the business objectives?
Message	4 How can you simplify your message?
	5 Is the message reasonable, do-able, and time-stamped? Is the language simple and clear? Have you used plain English? Would a picture, chart, table or diagram be more effective?
Audience	6 Who is your audience?
	7 What is particular about that audience?
	8 How credible are you with that audience?
Behavioural change	9 How can you say it in a clear, simple way? Is the message reasonable, do-able, and time-stamped? Is the language simple and clear? Have you used plain English? Would a picture, chart, table or diagram be more effective?
Context	10 Is the company thick or flat, centralised or decentralised? Are there any undiscussables? What kind of communication is normal? What kind is unacceptable?
Channels	11 Which channels work best for the audience and the purpose?
	12 Could different channels be used?
Filters and barriers	13 What barriers to understanding exist? Are there any physical or mental barriers to understanding, such as deafness, poor sight or ability? Are there language or cultural differences?
Supporting facts or examples	14 What facts/examples will bring your message to life and make it credible?
Business relevance	15 How can you link your message to a business objective?
Understanding check	16 How will you follow up to make sure the audience received your message as you intended?

Key question: What is my personality type?

Any sort of 360-degree feedback programme that assesses your personality and communication skills will give you the questions you need to ask about your personal communications skills. Common indicators are the Myers–Briggs Indicator®, DISC, Personalysis, the Birkman method and Keirsey–Bates Temperament Assessment Indicator. Understanding yourself, the listener, the message and its context are all important aspects of effective communication. Completing an assessment – whether formal or informal – will help you build understanding of your communication strengths and weaknesses and also answer vital questions about how well you communicate in your current business context.

The majority of personality and communication style assessments work along the same lines. The outcome of the assessment, whether formal or informal, identifies your patterns of communication according to 'typical' characteristics. Some assume we have a little of all; others assume we may be mostly one, without the others. All assume that one of the aspects identified in the assessment predominates in each of us. Each different aspect or perspective represents a different 'temperament' or hard-wiring on which various types of personality 'software' run. The assumption underlying the assessment is that we are not born as blank slates, but that we are 'wired' from birth to prefer certain ways of relating to people and perceiving the world, and how we make decisions and pass judgements.

The meaning or interpretation of an assessment can give you information about yourself and others' preferences. Most assessments assume that four characteristics form the basic circuits of our 'hardware'. The idea is not to stereotype anyone, but rather to provide you with information. Only you can decide just how useful or accurate it is. Typical categories arising from assessments relate to how we prefer to relate to the world, how we perceive information, how we make decisions, and how we actually relate to the world.

> 👍 **Applying the knowledge you gain from one of these assessments can help you become a more effective communicator because it can help you see how you and the people around you are 'wired'.**

Key question: What is my communication style?

Once you have gained some insight into your personality and temperament preferences, you can imagine how advantageous it can be to know your communication style so you can adapt your communication to get the desired response from those around you. So the questions you need to ask are all the ones in a typical communication style survey, addressed to all the people with whom you regularly communicate at work.

If you have no access to a communication style inventory, try asking a few simple questions of key stakeholders:

- What are my strengths as a communicator?
- What are my weaknesses as a communicator?
- Where or how does my communication need to improve?
- How would you recommend that I improve my communication?
- What is an example of my effective communication?
- What is an example of my ineffective communication?

By getting the answers to these questions, you should be able to work on your weaknesses and build on your strengths. The aim: to get the desired business results. I am not talking about manipulation here, but rather accepting that management communication is 'successful' only when you get the desired response from people. Knowing communication styles will help you recognise when clashes are just the result of frictions in style. You should try to get familiar with common styles, look for them in your workplace and learn to work with them for the mutual benefit of all concerned.

Many of us naturally think of communication as a written or spoken exchange between two people. But the reality is, alas, far more complex, as we learned earlier in this book. Communication involves, not just what we say, but how we say it, what our body language conveys and even how we dress or organise our personal space. The man sitting behind the cluttered desk wearing a rumpled shirt is telling us something about himself. The woman in the impeccable grey suit behind a desk with only a laptop and a phone is telling us something completely different.

Each of the four forms of communication play a role in our ability to send and receive messages. Verbal is the easiest form to control, but you need to be thinking about how others are interpreting your messages on the bases of your paraverbal, body language and personal space messaging.

Key question: What are we doing regarding employee communications?

Anyone who has been involved in employee communication knows that measurement is one of the most important aspects of employee communication. But in many companies, much of that measurement looks at whether employees access the tools organisations use to communicate with them, not how effective the strategy is as a whole, or how effective the messages are.

Common employee measurement questions include:

- Do they access the newsletter? Do they read it?
- Do they access the corporate blog?
- Do they find our intranet information webcasts interesting?

But it's very hard – impossible, some say – to prove that your employee communication tools measure engagement, which is, after all, what every CEO wants to know.

There is one key reason for this. You are only measuring the acceptance of communication tools, not measuring your employee communication strategy. So here's what you do.

What does your communications audit tell you? Every organisation conducts market research surveys. These surveys typically measure customer satisfaction levels across services and products provided by your organisation. Sometimes they even ask questions about competitor products and services. Organisations then take that information and work towards improving the rating they received by introducing improvements to services, products and information.

Now, many organisations have a human resources department that usually conducts a staff survey annually. This survey typically includes questions about communication within the organisation, understanding the corporate vision, satisfaction with employee benefits and training and so on.

What I suggest is that organisations include a supplementary survey of just 10 questions at the end of such a survey. And these questions should be framed by selecting key questions from the customer survey and asking staff what they think about key areas of communication. Refer to the section about meeting employee expectations (the six key questions on page 90). These questions become your employee communication engagement measure.

Typically the results demonstrate a disparity between what managers think and what employees think managers think. Once you have measured the difference between perception and reality you have the opportunity to start a dialogue with your employees about what they really expect from their managers' communication.

Most importantly, this allows you to design employee communication strategies specifically to target that business issue. So now you have a business measure and know the key messages that will form the basis of your employee communication strategy.

One year later when the employee survey has been conducted, you ask the same questions and again do the same with the staff survey. What you seek to find out is whether the measures of staff perception regarding what the organisation thinks employees think and what employees actually think have moved closer together and towards the organisation's desired communication outcome. This becomes your business measure of whether you have engaged employees with your communication.

This information is important because your ultimate aim in employee communication has to be to create the 'aha moment'. The aha moment is based on information that challenges an employee's belief about an aspect of the business. The information that suddenly helps employees say: 'Now it makes sense', 'Now I understand', 'Now I can do something about it'.

It is only once you see this gap close between what employees actually think about an issue and what employees think their managers think that you have a measure that demonstrates your employee communication engagement strategy has been successful. If the gap still exists then the design of your employee communication strategy is flawed in some way.

Finally, it is important that you measure employee communication tools such as readership of your staff magazine, access of your intranet and other tools. However, the only way to affect perceptions of the value that management communication contributes to an organisation is to measure communication and engagement strategies against business outcomes.

This approach to measurement is low cost. The investment in the human resources staff survey and the marketing department's customer research is already locked in. You are simply adding 10 communications strategy questions to the end of the human resources/employee engagement survey.

The engagement strategies are generally low cost because they involve people, not tools. By this I mean that employees are involved in doing something differently to bring about change in an organisation. The staff newsletter and other information tools already exist – all you do is tailor the articles to reflect the main focus of your employee engagement strategy.

This low-cost yet highly effective approach will ensure that you can measure your employee communication strategies against business outcomes.

Key questions to ask in a communications audit

General questions

1 Does management comprehend and fully support the premise that the company needs a high degree of communications? (Too often, management discovers the need for communication by having to respond to the lack of it.)
2 Does management have the effective skills in communication, including basic skills in listening, speaking, questioning and sharing feedback? Do employees get the feeling that we're hearing from them and they're hearing from us?
3 Do we have sound meeting management skills?
4 Do we have sound conflict communication skills?
5 Does everyone in the company feel comfortable with asserting that they don't understand a communication or suggesting when and how someone could communicate more effectively?

Policy and procedure questions

1 Does every employee have a copy of the strategic plan, which includes the organisation's mission, vision, values statement, strategic goals and strategies about how those goals will be reached?
2 Does every employee have an employee handbook that contains all up-to-date personnel policies?
3 Do we have a set of procedures for how routine tasks are conducted and include them in the standard operating manual?
4 Does every employee have a copy of their job description and the organisation chart?

Downward communication

1 Do we hold management meetings (at least every two weeks), even if there's nothing pressing to report? If you hold meetings only when you believe there's something to report, then communications will occur only when you have something to say – communications will be one-way and the organisation will suffer.

2 Do we hold full staff meetings every month to report on how the organisation is doing, major accomplishments, concerns, announcements about staff, etc.?

3 Do all our managers have face-to-face contact with employees at least once a week? Or if they are widely distributed around the globe, regularly, by video conference or teleconference?

4 Do we regularly hold meetings to celebrate major accomplishments? This helps employees perceive what's important, gives them a sense of direction and fulfilment, and lets them know that management is on top of things.

5 Do all employees have yearly performance reviews, which articulate their goals for the year, updated job descriptions, accomplishments, needs for improvement, and plans to help the employees accomplish the improvements?

6 Do all employees have a career and development plan?

Upward communication

1 Do all employees give regular status reports to their managers? This should include a section on what they did last week, will do next week and any actions/issues to address.

2 Do all managers meet one-on-one at least once a month with their employees to discuss how things are going, hear any current concerns from the employee, etc.? Even if the meeting is chit-chat, it cultivates an important relationship between supervisor and employee.

3 Does the company use management and staff meetings to solicit feedback, not just report? Ask how it's going. Use a round table approach to hear from each person.

4 Do managers act on feedback from others? Do you write feedback down? Get back to it – if only to say you can't do anything about the reported problem or suggestion, etc.?

5 Do you/does your company 'respect the grapevine'? It's probably one of the most prevalent and reliable forms of communication. Major 'movements' in the organisation usually first appear when employees feel that it's safe to venture their feelings or opinions to peers.

What levers should I pull?

The best way you can get anyone in your organisation to improve their communication is to create a communications plan and then measure its success. If you show the gaps between your desired communication objectives and your actual communication situation, you stand a better chance of getting people to improve their communications. This measurement is the only way you'll have any ammunition to argue for a change in communication methods.

The basics of such a plan are pretty straightforward. No matter what the steps are called, if you take the time to create an organised plan before you launch any communications, you will have a greater chance of succeeding and of learning for the future. The plan can be dynamic and change as the situation changes, but if a well-thought-out communications plan is in place before the campaign is launched, everyone involved will be better prepared to adapt to changes as they occur. Many companies (or the agencies that create their plans) have their own templates and 'house style'. Some are extremely short and simple, while others are lengthy and elaborate. The names may vary, but all communications plans should have six basic elements.

Your biggest lever: a strategic communications plan

1 Analysis of situation

Provide brief background information on the situation you're communicating about. For external communications plans, include information such as the company's history and current culture, the state of the marketplace or industry and the economic and political situation surrounding the company at the moment. Don't make the situational analysis too detailed. Include research the communications staff have access to or have done themselves, relevant studies and articles, expert testimony – even anecdotes from relevant employees' personal experience can be included. Provide a detailed portrait of the problem or opportunity.

2 Key messages

Articulate three succinct points or statements that the company, CEO or department would like to get across to its audiences. Write them out, in one sentence each.

3 Goals plus objectives

List the three major outcomes of the communications you want to accomplish with your communications plan. Write these goals in broad outline – more visionary than specific. Link the goals tightly to business objectives!

Each goal should then have one or two objectives. These must be specific and *measurable*. Always include milestones or a time stamp. For example, if one goal is 'to become the top iPAD dealer in our 10-county region' then one objective might be 'to increase sales of the iPAD in 2011 by 15 per cent over 2010 sales'.

Objectives are clearly measurable through quantitative research, such as studies and financial analyses. In the example above, it is easy to find out how many iPADS were sold in 2010, to track progress toward the 2011 goal, and to measure sales again at the end of 2011 to see if the objective was met.

4 Audiences

List the people (or entities) to whom you will communicate the key messages in order to reach the goals and objectives. Audiences are often divided into primary and secondary categories, especially when the budget is tight – so that staff can concentrate effort on the most important audiences first.

Think carefully about the audiences. With that said, give the choice of audiences careful thought. An audience includes anyone who might be affected by whatever the company is doing in this plan. For example, if the company is reorganising, people working in affected departments need to know. If the company is building a new genetics research lab the people living in the neighbourhood near the new site will need to receive some communication. An environmental group might become an audience if the facility is being built near a wildlife habitat. What's critical here is to leave no one out.

5 Tactics/channels

Come up with at least one communications tactic – the method you will use to communicate. For example, if your company's own employees are an audience, tactics might include an all-employee email message and an article in the employee newsletter; for board members, a letter from the CEO; for the media, a letter to the editor or a standard press release; and for the local community, an opinion piece in the local paper and a town hall meeting.

Deciding what tactics to use for each audience can be a challenge. Use research, your own experience and that of co-workers, advice from PR practitioners and industry best practices to determine how you can most effectively inform and persuade each audience.

6 Evaluation

You must include, at the end of every communication campaign, some form of evaluation. Define this evaluation in your plan. Even if the campaign's budget is tight, your relevant colleagues can do an informal review and discuss what went well and what didn't.

If you set clear, measurable objectives when you developed your plan, you should be able to run some sort of research (see Chapter 8 on measurement) to determine whether you reached your objectives. Collect feedback from various audiences, whether informally through emails, calls or a review of media coverage of the issue, or formally with a scientific survey done at the beginning of the campaign and repeated at the end.

There are dozens of ways to evaluate the success of your communications, whether through the ongoing 'campaign' I've been advocating, or one clearly defined campaign. None of them is necessarily 'right' or 'wrong'.

 The only mistake you can make if you care about communication is to fail to evaluate the campaign at all.

How do we know when we've succeed or failed?

Simple: measure and evaluate.

- Ask the people you communicate with.
- Do audits, surveys and focus groups, and have informal chats in the company restaurant.
- Do a employee communications audit.
- Ask your stakeholders how well your department, division or company is communicating.
- Get some kind of 360-degree feedback on your own communication performance.

Success or failure in communication depends on the objective of the communication. Most effective communicators work from a plan. Depending on the scope of the communication – from a face-to-face conversation to a major external company PR campaign – this plan will vary.

Many effective management communicators can practically make this 'plan' in their heads. It's second nature. They know their audience, can tell you the purpose, understand the best way to convey the message, can articulate the key message in one sentence and have good enough relationships with their people that they 'know' if they succeeded by listening and getting feedback in one of the myriad ways we covered earlier. For larger internal or external campaigns that involve many audiences and purposes, and a series of messages, with a variety of channels and staggered timing, determining success or failure means doing some sort of research.

One common formula for communications planning is RACE:

- **Research** — Investigate and describe the communication situation and the need for communications.
- **Analyse** — Determine the target audience, goals and objectives and communications tactics.
- **Communicate** – Implement the tactics.
- **Evaluate** – Determine your level of success in achieving the plan's goals and objectives.

If you do your homework during the first three steps (R, A, C) – especially the first (R) – you will find the final step (E) relatively easy. And you will know quickly whether you have succeeded or failed. In a perfect world, you could basically repeat the research done in the first step at the end of the campaign to evaluate its success. Of course, you don't live in a perfect world, and you don't always have the time, people resources and budget to conduct full-fledged scientifically valid research studies for a communications campaign. But you do have the resources, at least informally, to check for understanding, as we suggested in the section above.

Research and evaluation are usually given less time, money and effort than goal-setting and the actual communications tactics. Many managers wrongly believe that research is inherently too expensive and difficult for smaller or non-profit organisations. They equate 'research' with doing a scientific survey. In fact, there is a wide range of valid research techniques available – many of which are 'free' (except for the time investment).

How do you know what method to use?

Use your judgement. Examine the situation and determine how much time and money you have and what other resources are available (e.g. co-workers, temps, volunteers). Ask yourself how important this communication project is to your organisation in terms of potential impact on sales, finances or people.

- Is this a massive new product launch that could make or break the company?
- Is this your primary advertising and PR campaign taking up most of your communications budget for the year?
- Is this a speech announcing a major, two-year reorganisation or acquisition that affects the lives of every single employee in your 18,000-person organisation?

It might suffice to give a report to a small company's board of directors using mostly informal research. They will understand and appreciate your time and budget constraints. On the other hand, if you have to report on this campaign to your CEO on behalf of your whole department, or division, it might be worth the money and effort to do some serious, original primary research.

When you draft your communications plan, set measurable objectives based on your initial research. This research, your objectives and your evaluation methods should be tied closely together. For example, you might conduct a focus group to determine a certain audience's attitudes during the research phase of your campaign, then design and implement a telephone survey based on the results of your focus groups. After you have implemented your campaign, you should be able to repeat one or both of these methods in the evaluation phase to determine whether you have met your objectives.

A typical employee engagement and communication survey

1 Has your organisation's communication budget and/or human resources budget changed in the past 12 months?
   - Budget
   - Staff

2 What are the reasons for the changes in the size?
   - Mandated cuts
   - Economic downturn
   - Shifting resources
   - Bankruptcy
   - Reorganisation
   - Merger or acquisition
   - Growth
   - Increase workload
   - Staff attrition
   - Other

3 Which of these communications methods does your organisation use to engage employees and foster productivity?
   - Business television
   - Emails
   - Face-to-face-meetings
   - Targeted mailing
   - Intranet
   - Podcasts
   - Posters/flyers
   - Printed employee newsletters or newspaper
   - Social media
   - Town hall meetings
   - Videos

- Virtual meetings
- Website
- Other

4   How often does your organisation perform ongoing employee 'listening' through surveys, focus groups and other research methods?
- Weekly
- Monthly
- Quarterly
- Semi-annually
- Annually
- Rarely
- Never

5   What kinds of internal or external social media tools does your organisation currently use?
- Audio podcasts
- Blogs
- Discussion boards
- Facebook
- Flickr
- Instant messaging
- Internal social networks
- MySpace
- RSS feeds
- Twitter
- Vidcasts
- Wikis
- Yammer
- YouTube
- Other

6   Has your organisation developed a policy to address employee use of internal social media?

....

7   Do top executives in your organisation participate actively in the use of internal social media tools?
- Usage/statistic monitoring
- Gathering anecdotes or case studies
- Information monitoring

8   Has your organisation developed a policy to address employee use of external social media?

....

9 Do top executives in your organisation participate actively in the use of external social media tools, and if so, how frequently?
- Yes – regularly
- Yes – occasionally
- Not at this time

10 What methods, if any, does your organisation use to measure the effectiveness of external social media tools?
- Web traffic
- Page views
- Blogs and other mentions
- Downloads
- Technorati, Google, Radian6
- Google analytics, web trends
- Attitude (share of conversation, tonality of comments, measure relationships, net promoter scope)
- Measuring actions and business results (cost comparisons, revenue, subscribers, sales)

How leaders and managers value communication

11 To what extent are senior leaders (including the CEO, if applicable) and managers partnering with or relying on internal communicators to ensure effective communication throughout your organisation?
- They partner with communicators more frequently now than 12 months ago.
- Same frequency
- They don't partner

12 Did your organisation's employee engagement strategy change after the global economic downturn began?
- We are communicating less
- More
- Stayed the same

Engagement, recognition, performance

13 Has your organisation seen a return on its communication investment in terms of employee retention in the past 12 months?
- Strongly agree
- Agree
- Neutral

14 To what factors would you attribute your organisation's gain or loss in employee retention?
- Amount of employee communication
- Change in leadership

- Change in company ownership
- Downsizing
- Economic downturn
- Retention bonuses
- Retirement
- Poor management/leadership
- Poor morale
- Differentiate benefits

Creating and sustaining a culture of engagement

15 How important was each of the following goals in your company's decisions to develop programmes and strategies for engaging employees in [YEAR].

16 Create a new culture or work environment: extremely important/very important/moderately important/slightly important/not at all important
- Increase employee morale
- Increase productivity
- Reduce disciplinary issue among workforce
- Retain top talent
- Transfer knowledge to younger employees

17 List any other goals that may have had an influence on programmes and strategies for engaging employees:

....

....

18 Which of the following practices does your company use to create and sustain its desired work culture?
- Publish a formal list of values or description of the desired culture
- Include material on the organisation's culture in new-hire orientation
- Involve senior leadership in orientation programmes to transmit visions, values and culture
- Regularly survey your workforce on engagement and work satisfaction
- Proved a 'career portal' website for employees to identify opportunities for advancement
- Use 'exit interviews' with managers leaving the organisation
- Other

19 How is your company measuring the effectiveness of its employee engagement strategies?
- Formal or informal employee feedback
- Measurable employee retention rates
- Meeting annual company performance goals
- Increased employee participation in benefit programmes
- Improved new-hire percentages
- Other

Management development programmes

20 Which of the following management development programmes or practices do you use?
- Formal mentoring programmes
- Formal 'new hire' orientation or 'boot camp' programmes
- Leadership training (in addition to routine 'management' training)
- Required formal development plans
- Hold managers accountable for developing action plans based on employee survey results
- Assess progress on meeting development plan goal as part of the employee review process
- Provide defined opportunities for advancement (e.g. career paths) with clear guidelines and expectations
- Training on supportive communications, interpersonal skills, team-building, collaborative problem solving and other 'soft skills'
- Training on conducting performance reviews and feedback sessions
- Provide special career development programmes for high-potential managers
- Use professional personality assessments as part of the management development process
- Train managers in goal-setting

21 Which of the following performance management activities or practices do you use?
- Conduct formal performance reviews on your employees at least once a year
- Jointly set goals with your employees
- Assess the consistency between a manager's behaviour and the cultural values of the organisation
- Regularly use recognition and reward ceremonies to celebrate achievements

22 Please describe the performance management programme, practice or activity that you think has been most important in increasing the level of employee engagement in your organisation:

....

....

Internal employer branding

23 Does your organisation have a well-established internal employer brand?

....

24 Are the key messages (values, etc.) behind your internal brand reinforced in most of your internal communication, as appropriate?

....

 *Briefing Lessons*

To avoid the pitfalls of short-term, reactive communication, managers should:

- Make a commitment to long-term, purposeful strategic communication.
- Create a long-term strategic communications plan, for at least the next 12 months, with three to five key messages for each important stakeholder group.
- Conceive of every communication as part of a three-step process: preparing, sending the message, checking for understanding.
- Remember to evaluate the impact of their communication (many managers give this step short shrift).

The chapter showed:

- How to improve strategic communication in three areas of communication: interpersonal, internal and external.
- What questions to ask in order to improve every communication.
- How to determine the impact of your personality style and your communication style on your communication.
- How to assess the quality of your company's communication processes.
- How to improve your employee communications with an audit (including sample questions).

[PART FOUR]

In depth

Additional resources

11

- Books
- Online references
- Courses

Books

Business research

Applied Business Research: Qualitative and Quantitative Methods, Cavana, Delahaye and Sekaran, Wiley and Sons, 2001.
Research Methods for Business: A Skill Building Approach, Sekaran, John Wiley and Sons, 2000.

Speaking skills

Give Your Speech, Change the World: How to Move Your Audience To Action, Morgan, HBS Press, 2003.
Presentation Zen: Simple Ideas on Presentation Design and Delivery, Reynolds, New Riders, 2008.
Say It With Presentations: How To Design and Deliver Successful Presentations, Zelazny, McGraw-Hill, 2006.
How To Make An Impact: Influence, Inform and Impress With Your Reports, Presentations and Business Documents, Moon, FT Prentice Hall, 2008.

Management communication

The Art of Woo: Using Strategic Persuasion to Sell Your Ideas, Shell and Moussa, Portfolio, 2007.
Business Communication, Harvard Business Essentials, HBS Press, 2003.
Changing Minds: The Art and Science of Changing Our Own and Other People's Minds, Gardner, HBS Press, 2006.
Communicating at Work: Principles and Practices for Business and the Professions, Adler and Elmhorts, McGraw-Hill, 2002.
Corporate Communication: A Strategic Approach to Building Reputation, Bronn and Berg (eds.), Gyldendal, 2005.
Guide To Managerial Communication, Munter, Prentice Hall, 2006.
The Jelly Effect: How to Make Your Communications Stick, Bounds, Capstone, 2007.
Leadership Presence: Dramatic Techniques to Reach Out, Motivate and Inspire, Halpern and Lubar, Gotham Books, 2003.
Made to Stick: Why Some Ideas Survive and Others Die, Heath and Heath, Random House, 2007.
Management Communication, Bell and Smith, John Wiley and Sons, 2010.
Words That Work: It's Not What You Say, It's What People Hear, Luntz, Hyperion, 2007.
Why Business People Speak Like Idiots: A Bullfighter's Guide, Fugere, Hardaway and Warshawsky, Free Press, 2005.

Online references

Harvard Business Review (also a monthly magazine) (http://hbr.org). Excellent articles that relate to communication in almost every issue.
McKinsey Quarterly (www.mckinseyquarterly.com). Excellent articles on a wide range of management topics, including the occasional piece on communication, branding, reputation, marketing, electronic media.
International Association of Business Communicators (www.iabc.com). Excellent online resource for all matters of communication. Aimed at communications professionals, but useful for all managers who are interested in communication.
TED (www.TED.com). Ideas worth spreading: riveting talks by remarkable people, free of charge.

Courses

Management Centre Europe (MCE). http://www.mce-ama.com/

Index

SharePoint 106
sharing information 8
situational analysis 166
slides 56–7, 59
SMART messages 52–5, 79
social networking channels 100–7, 150
    collaboration technology 106
    file transfer protocol 105, 149
    instant messaging 103
    personal digital assistant (PDA) 103
    presence software 107
    teleconferencing 104
    telepresence 107
    unified communications 106
    videoconferencing 104
    web conferencing 105
    wiki 105, 150
SoftWin 110–11
speech 70
spheres of communication 32–3
stage fright 40
stakeholder communications 132, 150
stakeholder map 97–8
stories 60–3, 63, 116, 128–31, 149
storyboard 58
strategic communication 5–6, 14, 36, 114
strategic messages 95–6
strategic planning 109–11, 131–4, 148
    evaluation 167–8
    RACE formula 169
    success or failure 168–9
strategic questions 79
stress 83
structure 58
style of communication 107–9, 161–2
sub-group map 46
subtext 11, 49
success attribution 48, 168–9

surveys 140, 163, 170–5
symptoms of poor communication 156

tactics 167
teams 20, 48
TED.com 56
telecommuting 101
teleconferencing 104
telepresence 107
Tetra Pak 95
three-step model 6, 36, 82
tone 51
Toyota 28–30, 126–7
Transoceanic 125
Trillian 103
trust 18, 85–6
Twitter 102
two-way model 123–4

underlying meaning 11
understanding 11–12, 67–76, 80, 109
undiscussable topics 49
unified communications 106
upward communication 165

values 21, 49
venue for presentations 59
videoconferencing 104
vision 27
voice of the company 115
voice volume 70

web conferencing 105
Webex 105
websites 124–5
wiki 105, 150
women 48
writing skills 19